EQUAL CREDIT OPPORTUNITY ACT

FAIR DEBT COLLECTION PRACTICES ACT

ELECTRONIC FUND TRANSFER ACT

15 U.S.C. §§ 1691-1693r, as amended

Revised
January 2024

CONTENTS

EQUAL CREDIT OPPORTUNITY ACT

15 U.S.C. §§ 1691-1691f, as amended

This Act (Title VII of the Consumer Credit Protection Act) prohibits discrimination on the basis of race, color, religion, national origin, sex, marital status, age, receipt of public assistance, or good faith exercise of any rights under the Consumer Credit Protection Act. The Act also requires creditors to provide applicants, upon request, with the reasons underlying decisions to deny credit. The Dodd-Frank Act added, among other things, a requirement that creditors provide to applicants a copy of all appraisals and other written valuations used in connection with the applicant's application for first lien loans secured by a dwelling.

Revised
January 2024

SUBCHAPTER IV—EQUAL CREDIT OPPORTUNITY

§1691. Scope of prohibition

(a) Activities constituting discrimination

It shall be unlawful for any creditor to discriminate against any applicant, with respect to any aspect of a credit transaction—

(1) on the basis of race, color, religion, national origin, sex or marital status, or age (provided the applicant has the capacity to contract);

(2) because all or part of the applicant's income derives from any public assistance program; or

(3) because the applicant has in good faith exercised any right under this chapter.

(b) Activities not constituting discrimination

It shall not constitute discrimination for purposes of this subchapter for a creditor—

(1) to make an inquiry of marital status if such inquiry is for the purpose of ascertaining the creditor's rights and remedies applicable to the particular extension of credit and not to discriminate in a determination of credit-worthiness;

(2) to make an inquiry of the applicant's age or of whether the applicant's income derives from any public assistance program if such inquiry is for the purpose of determining the amount and probable continuance of income levels, credit history, or other pertinent element of credit-worthiness as provided in regulations of the Bureau;

(3) to use any empirically derived credit system which considers age if such system is demonstrably and statistically sound in accordance with regulations of the Bureau, except that in the operation of such system the age of an elderly applicant may not be assigned a negative factor or value;

(4) to make an inquiry or to consider the age of an elderly applicant when the age of such applicant is to be used by the creditor in the extension of credit in favor of such applicant; or

(5) to make an inquiry under section 1691c–2 of this title, in accordance with the requirements of that section.

(c) Additional activities not constituting discrimination

It is not a violation of this section for a creditor to refuse to extend credit offered pursuant to—

(1) any credit assistance program expressly authorized by law for an economically disadvantaged class of persons;

(2) any credit assistance program administered by a nonprofit organization for its members or an economically disadvantaged class of persons; or

(3) any special purpose credit program offered by a profit-making organization to meet special social needs which meets standards prescribed in regulations by the Bureau;

if such refusal is required by or made pursuant to such program.

(d) Reason for adverse action; procedure applicable; "adverse action" defined

(1) Within thirty days (or such longer reasonable time as specified in regulations of the Bureau for any class of credit transaction) after receipt of a completed application for credit, a creditor shall notify the applicant of its action on the application.

(2) Each applicant against whom adverse action is taken shall be entitled to a statement of reasons for such action from the creditor. A creditor satisfies this obligation by—

(A) providing statements of reasons in writing as a matter of course to applicants against whom adverse action is taken; or

(B) giving written notification of adverse action which discloses (i) the applicant's right to a statement of reasons within thirty days after receipt by the creditor of a request made within sixty days after such notification, and (ii) the identity of the person or office from which such statement may be obtained. Such statement may be given orally if the written notification advises the applicant of his right to have the statement of reasons confirmed in writing on written request.

(3) A statement of reasons meets the requirements of this section only if it contains the specific reasons for the adverse action taken.

(4) Where a creditor has been requested by a third party to make a specific extension of credit directly or indirectly to an applicant, the notification and statement of reasons required by this subsection may be made directly by such creditor, or indirectly through the third party, provided in either case that the identity of the creditor is disclosed.

(5) The requirements of paragraph (2), (3), or (4) may be satisfied by verbal statements or notifications in the case of any creditor who did not act on more than one hundred and fifty applications during the calendar year preceding the calendar year in which the adverse action is taken, as determined under regulations of the Bureau.

(6) For purposes of this subsection, the term "adverse action" means a denial or revocation of credit, a change in the terms of an existing credit arrangement, or a refusal to grant credit in substantially the amount or on substantially the terms requested. Such term does not include a refusal to extend additional credit under an existing credit arrangement where the applicant is delinquent or otherwise in default, or where such additional credit would exceed a previously established credit limit.

(e) Copies furnished to applicants

(1) In general

Each creditor shall furnish to an applicant a copy of any and all written appraisals and valuations developed in connection with the applicant's application for a loan that is secured or would have been secured by a first lien on a dwelling promptly upon completion, but in no case later than 3 days prior to the closing of the loan, whether the creditor grants or denies the applicant's request for credit or the application is incomplete or withdrawn.

(2) Waiver

The applicant may waive the 3 day requirement provided for in paragraph (1), except where otherwise required in law.

(3) Reimbursement

The applicant may be required to pay a reasonable fee to reimburse the creditor for the cost of the appraisal, except where otherwise required in law.

(4) Free copy

Notwithstanding paragraph (3), the creditor shall provide a copy of each written appraisal or valuation at no additional cost to the applicant.

(5) Notification to applicants

At the time of application, the creditor shall notify an applicant in writing of the right to receive a copy of each written appraisal and valuation under this subsection.

(6) Valuation defined

For purposes of this subsection, the term "valuation" shall include any estimate of the value of a dwelling developed in connection with a creditor's decision to provide credit, including those values developed pursuant to a policy of a government sponsored enterprise or by an automated valuation model, a broker price opinion, or other methodology or mechanism.

(Pub. L. 90–321, title VII, §701, as added Pub. L. 93–495, title V, §503, Oct. 28, 1974, 88 Stat. 1521; amended Pub. L. 94–239, §2, Mar. 23, 1976, 90 Stat. 251; Pub. L. 102–242, title II, §223(d), Dec. 19, 1991, 105 Stat. 2306; Pub. L. 111–203, title X, §§1071(b), 1085(1), title XIV, §1474, July 21, 2010, 124 Stat. 2059, 2083, 2199.)

EDITORIAL NOTES

AMENDMENTS

2010—Pub. L. 111–203, §1085(1), substituted "Bureau" for "Board" wherever appearing.

Subsec. (b)(5). Pub. L. 111–203, §1071(b), added par. (5).

Subsec. (e). Pub. L. 111–203, §1474, amended subsec. (e) generally. Prior to amendment, subsec. (e) read as follows: "Each creditor shall promptly furnish an applicant, upon written request by the applicant made within a reasonable period of time of the application, a copy of the appraisal report used in connection with the applicant's application for a loan that is or would have been secured by a lien on residential real property. The creditor may require the applicant to reimburse the creditor for the cost of the appraisal."

1991—Subsec. (e). Pub. L. 102–242 added subsec. (e).

1976—Subsec. (a). Pub. L. 94–239 designated existing provisions as cl. (1), expanded prohibition against discrimination to include race, color, religion, national origin and age, and added cls. (2) and (3).

Subsec. (b). Pub. L. 94–239 designated existing provisions as cl. (1) and added cls. (2) to (4).

Subsecs. (c), (d). Pub. L. 94–239 added subsecs. (c) and (d).

STATUTORY NOTES AND RELATED SUBSIDIARIES

Pub. L. 111–203, title X, §1071(d), July 21, 2010, 124 Stat. 2059, provided that: "This section [enacting section 1691o–2 of this title and amending this section] shall become effective on the designated transfer date."

[The term "designated transfer date" is defined in section 5481(9) of Title 12, Banks and Banking, as the date established under section 5582 of Title 12.]

Amendment by section 1085(1) of Pub. L. 111–203 effective on the designated transfer date, see section 1100H of Pub. L. 111–203, set out as a note under section 552a of Title 5, Government Organization and Employees.

Amendment by section 1474 of Pub. L. 111–203 effective on the date on which final regulations implementing that amendment take effect, or on the date that is 18 months after the designated transfer date if such regulations have not been issued by that date, see section 1400(c) of Pub. L. 111–203, set out as a note under section 1601 of this title.

EFFECTIVE DATE

Section 708, formerly §707, of title VII of Pub. L. 90–321, as added by Pub. L. 93–495, title V, §503, Oct. 28, 1974, 88 Stat. 1525, renumbered and amended by Pub. L. 94–239, §§7, 8, Mar. 23, 1976, 90 Stat. 255, provided that: "This title [enacting this subchapter and provisions set out as notes under section 1691 of this title] takes effect upon the expiration of one year after the date of its enactment [Oct. 28, 1974]. The amendments made by the Equal Credit Opportunity Act Amendments of 1976 [enacting section 1691f of this title, amending this section and sections 1691b, 1691c, 1691d, and 1691e of this title, repealing section 1609 of this title, enacting provisions set out as notes under this section, and repealing provisions set out as a note under this section] shall take effect on the date of enactment thereof [Mar. 23, 1976] and shall apply to any violation occurring on or after such date, except that the amendments made to section 701 of the Equal Credit Opportunity Act [this section] shall take effect 12 months after the date of enactment [Mar. 23, 1976]."

SHORT TITLE

This subchapter known as the "Equal Credit Opportunity Act", see Short Title note set out under section 1601 of this title.

CONGRESSIONAL FINDINGS AND STATEMENT OF PURPOSE

Pub. L. 93–495, title V, §502, Oct. 28, 1974, 88 Stat. 1521, provided that: "The Congress finds that there is a need to insure that the various financial institutions and other firms engaged in the extensions of credit exercise their responsibility to make credit available with fairness, impartiality, and without discrimination on the basis of sex or marital status. Economic stabilization would be enhanced and competition among the various financial institutions and other firms engaged in the extension of credit would be strengthened by an absence of discrimination on the basis of sex or marital status, as well as by the informed use of credit which Congress has heretofore sought to promote. It is the purpose of this Act [see Short Title note set out under section 1601 of this title] to require that financial institutions and other firms engaged in the extension of credit make that credit equally available to all credit-worthy customers without regard to sex or marital status."

§1691a. Definitions; rules of construction

(a) The definitions and rules of construction set forth in this section are applicable for the purposes of this subchapter.

(b) The term "applicant" means any person who applies to a creditor directly for an extension, renewal, or continuation of credit, or applies to a creditor indirectly by use of an existing credit plan for an amount exceeding a previously established credit limit.

(c) The term "Bureau" means the Bureau of Consumer Financial Protection.

(d) The term "credit" means the right granted by a creditor to a debtor to defer payment of debt or to incur debts and defer its payment or to purchase property or services and defer payment therefor.

(e) The term "creditor" means any person who regularly extends, renews, or continues credit; any person who regularly arranges for the extension, renewal, or continuation of credit; or any assignee of an original creditor who participates in the decision to extend, renew, or continue credit.

(f) The term "person" means a natural person, a corporation, government or governmental subdivision or agency, trust, estate, partnership, cooperative, or association.

(g) Any reference to any requirement imposed under this subchapter or any provision thereof includes reference to the regulations of the Bureau under this subchapter or the provision thereof in question.

(Pub. L. 90–321, title VII, §702, as added Pub. L. 93–495, title V, §503, Oct. 28, 1974, 88 Stat. 1522; amended Pub. L. 111–203, title X, §1085(1), (2), July 21, 2010, 124 Stat. 2083.)

EDITORIAL NOTES

AMENDMENTS

2010—Subsec. (c). Pub. L. 111–203, §1085(2), added subsec. (c) and struck out former subsec. (c) which read as follows: "The term 'Board' refers to the Board of Governors of the Federal Reserve System."

Subsec. (g). Pub. L. 111–203, §1085(1), substituted "Bureau" for "Board".

STATUTORY NOTES AND RELATED SUBSIDIARIES

EFFECTIVE DATE OF 2010 AMENDMENT

Amendment by Pub. L. 111–203 effective on the designated transfer date, see section 1100H of Pub. L. 111–203, set out as a note under section 552a of Title 5, Government Organization and Employees.

§1691b. Promulgation of regulations by the Bureau

(a) In general

The Bureau shall prescribe regulations to carry out the purposes of this subchapter. These regulations may contain but are not limited to such classifications, differentiation, or other provision, and may provide for such adjustments and exceptions for any class of transactions, as in the judgment of the Bureau are necessary or proper to effectuate the purposes of this subchapter, to prevent circumvention or evasion thereof, or to facilitate or substantiate compliance therewith.

(b) Exempt transactions

Such regulations may exempt from the provisions of this subchapter any class of transactions that are not primarily for personal, family, or household purposes, or business or commercial loans made available by a financial institution, except that a particular type within a class of such transactions may be exempted if the Bureau determines, after making an express finding that the application of this subchapter or of any provision of this subchapter of such transaction would not contribute substantially to effecting the purposes of this subchapter.

(c) Limitation on exemptions

An exemption granted pursuant to subsection (b) shall be for no longer than five years and shall be extended only if the Bureau makes a subsequent determination, in the manner described by such paragraph,[1] that such exemption remains appropriate.

(d) Maintenance of records

Pursuant to Bureau regulations, entities making business or commercial loans shall maintain such records or other data relating to such loans as may be necessary to evidence compliance with this subsection [2] or enforce any action pursuant to the authority of this chapter. In no event shall such records or data be maintained for a period of less than one year. The Bureau shall promulgate regulations to implement this paragraph [3] in the manner prescribed by chapter 5 of title 5.

(e) Notice of denial of loan

The Bureau shall provide in regulations that an applicant for a business or commercial loan shall be provided a written notice of such applicant's right to receive a written statement of the reasons for the denial of such loan.

(f) Board authority

Notwithstanding subsection (a), the Board shall prescribe regulations to carry out the purposes of this subchapter with respect to a person described in section 5519(a) of title 12. These regulations may contain but are not limited to such classifications, differentiation, or other provision, and may provide for such adjustments and exceptions for any class of transactions, as in the judgment of the Board are necessary or proper to effectuate the purposes of this subchapter, to prevent circumvention or evasion thereof, or to facilitate or substantiate compliance therewith.

(g) Deference

Notwithstanding any power granted to any Federal agency under this subchapter, the deference that a court affords to a Federal agency with respect to a determination made by such agency relating to the meaning or interpretation of any provision of this subchapter that is subject to the jurisdiction of such agency shall be applied as if that agency were the only agency authorized to apply, enforce, interpret, or administer the provisions of this subchapter [4]

(Pub. L. 90–321, title VII, §703, as added Pub. L. 93–495, title V, §503, Oct. 28, 1974, 88 Stat. 1522; amended Pub. L. 94–239, §3(a), Mar. 23, 1976, 90 Stat. 252; Pub. L. 100–533, title III, §301, Oct. 25, 1988, 102 Stat. 2692; Pub. L. 111–203, title X, §1085(1), (3), July 21, 2010, 124 Stat. 2083.)

Editorial Notes

Amendments

2010—Pub. L. 111–203, §1085(3)(A), substituted "Promulgation of regulations by the Bureau" for "Regulations" in section catchline.

Pub. L. 111–203, §1085(1), substituted "Bureau" for "Board" wherever appearing.

Subsecs. (a) to (e). Pub. L. 111–203, §1085(3)(B)–(E), in subsec. (a), struck out "(a)" designation before "(1)", redesignated subsec. (a) pars. (1) to (5) as subsecs. (a) to (e), respectively; in subsec. (c) substituted "subsection (b)" for "paragraph (2)", and struck out former subsec. (b), which related to establishment of a Consumer Advisory Council to advise and consult with the Board.

Subsecs. (f), (g). Pub. L. 111–203, §1085(3)(F), added subsecs. (f) and (g).

1988—Subsec. (a). Pub. L. 100–533 amended subsec. (a) generally. Prior to amendment, subsec. (a) read as follows: "The Board shall prescribe regulations to carry out the purposes of this subchapter. These regulations may contain but are not limited to such classifications, differentiation, or other provision, and may provide for such adjustments and exceptions for any class of transactions, as in the judgment of the Board are necessary or proper to effectuate the purposes of this subchapter, to prevent circumvention or evasion thereof, or to facilitate or substantiate compliance therewith. In particular, such regulations may exempt from one or more of the provisions of this subchapter any class of transactions not primarily for personal, family, or household purposes, if the Board makes an express finding that the application of such provision or provisions would not contribute substantially to carrying out the purposes of this subchapter. Such regulations shall be prescribed as soon as possible after the date of enactment of this Act, but in no event later than the effective date of this Act."

1976—Pub. L. 94–239 designated existing provisions as subsec. (a), inserted provisions exempting from regulations of this subchapter any class of transactions not primarily for personal, family, or household purposes to be determined by the Board, and added subsec. (b).

Statutory Notes and Related Subsidiaries

Effective Date of 2010 Amendment

Amendment by Pub. L. 111–203 effective on the designated transfer date, see section 1100H of Pub. L. 111–203, set out as a note under section 552a of Title 5, Government Organization and Employees.

Effective Date of 1976 Amendment

Amendment by Pub. L. 94–239 effective Mar. 23, 1976, see section 708 of Pub. L. 90–321, set out as an Effective Date note under section 1691 of this title.

[1] So in original. Probably should be "subsection."

[2] So in original.

[3] So in original. Probably should be "subsection".

[4] So in original. Probably should be followed by a period.

§1691c. Administrative enforcement

(a) Enforcing agencies

Subject to subtitle B of the Consumer Protection Financial Protection Act of 2010 [1] with [2] the requirements imposed under this subchapter shall be enforced under:

(1) section 8 of the Federal Deposit Insurance Act [12 U.S.C. 1818], by the appropriate Federal banking agency, as defined in section 3(q) of the Federal Deposit Insurance Act (12 U.S.C. 1813(q)), with respect to—

(A) national banks, Federal savings associations, and Federal branches and Federal agencies of foreign banks;

(B) member banks of the Federal Reserve System (other than national banks), branches and agencies of foreign banks (other than Federal branches, Federal agencies, and insured State branches of foreign banks), commercial lending companies owned or controlled by foreign banks, and organizations operating under section 25 or 25A of the Federal Reserve Act [12 U.S.C. 601 et seq., 611 et seq.]; and

(C) banks and State savings associations insured by the Federal Deposit Insurance Corporation (other than members of the Federal Reserve System), and insured State branches of foreign banks;

(2) The Federal Credit Union Act [12 U.S.C. 1751 et seq.], by the Administrator of the National Credit Union Administration with respect to any Federal Credit Union.

(3) Subtitle IV of title 49, by the Secretary of Transportation, with respect to all carriers subject to the jurisdiction of the Surface Transportation Board.

(4) Part A of subtitle VII of title 49, by the Secretary of Transportation with respect to any air carrier or foreign air carrier subject to that part.

(5) The Packers and Stockyards Act, 1921 [7 U.S.C. 181 et seq.] (except as provided in section 406 of that Act [7 U.S.C. 226, 227]), by the Secretary of Agriculture with respect to any activities subject to that Act.

(6) The Farm Credit Act of 1971 [12 U.S.C. 2001 et seq.], by the Farm Credit Administration with respect to any Federal land bank, Federal land bank association, Federal intermediate credit bank, and production credit association;

(7) The Securities Exchange Act of 1934 [15 U.S.C. 78a et seq.], by the Securities and Exchange Commission with respect to brokers and dealers;

(8) The Small Business Investment Act of 1958 [15 U.S.C. 661 et seq.], by the Small Business Administration, with respect to small business investment companies; and

(9) Subtitle E of the Consumer Financial Protection Act of 2010 [12 U.S.C. 5561 et seq.], by the Bureau, with respect to any person subject to this subchapter.

The terms used in paragraph (1) that are not defined in this subchapter or otherwise defined in section 3(s) of the Federal Deposit Insurance Act (12 U.S.C. 1813(s)) shall have the meaning given to them in section 1(b) of the International Banking Act of 1978 (12 U.S.C. 3101).

(b) Violations of subchapter deemed violations of preexisting statutory requirements; additional agency powers

For the purpose of the exercise by any agency referred to in subsection (a) of its powers under any Act referred to in that subsection, a violation of any requirement imposed under this subchapter shall be deemed to be a violation of a requirement imposed under that Act. In addition to its powers under any provision of law specifically referred to in subsection (a), each of the agencies referred to in that subsection may exercise for the purpose of enforcing compliance with any requirement imposed under this subchapter, any other authority conferred on it by law. The exercise of the authorities of any of the agencies referred to in subsection (a) for the purpose of enforcing compliance with any requirement imposed under this subchapter shall in no way preclude the exercise of such authorities for the purpose of enforcing compliance with any other provision of law not relating to the prohibition of discrimination on the basis of sex or marital status with respect to any aspect of a credit transaction.

(c) Overall enforcement authority of Federal Trade Commission

Except to the extent that enforcement of the requirements imposed under this subchapter is specifically committed to some other Government agency under any of paragraphs (1) through (8) of subsection (a), and subject to subtitle B of the Consumer Financial Protection Act of 2010, the Federal Trade Commission shall be authorized to enforce such requirements. For the purpose of the exercise by the Federal Trade Commission of its functions and powers under the Federal Trade Commission Act (15 U.S.C. 41 et seq.), a violation of any requirement imposed under this subchapter [3] shall be deemed a violation of a requirement imposed under that Act. All of the functions and powers of the Federal Trade Commission under the Federal Trade Commission Act are available to the Federal Trade Commission to enforce compliance by any person with the requirements imposed under this subchapter, irrespective of whether that person is engaged in commerce or meets any other jurisdictional tests under the Federal Trade Commission Act, including the power to enforce any rule prescribed by the Bureau under this subchapter in the same manner as if the violation had been a violation of a Federal Trade Commission trade regulation rule.

(d) Rules and regulations by enforcing agencies

The authority of the Bureau to issue regulations under this subchapter does not impair the authority of any other agency designated in this section to make rules respecting its own procedures in enforcing compliance with requirements imposed under this subchapter.

(Pub. L. 90–321, title VII, §704, as added Pub. L. 93–495, title V, §503, Oct. 28, 1974, 88 Stat. 1522; amended Pub. L. 94–239, §4, Mar. 23, 1976, 90 Stat. 253; Pub. L. 98–443, §9(n), Oct. 4, 1984, 98 Stat. 1708; Pub. L. 101–73, title VII, §744(m), Aug. 9, 1989, 103 Stat. 439; Pub. L. 102–242, title II, §212(d), Dec. 19, 1991, 105 Stat. 2300; Pub. L. 102–550, title XVI, §1604(a)(7), Oct. 28, 1992, 106 Stat. 4082; Pub. L. 104–88, title III, §315, Dec. 29, 1995, 109 Stat. 948; Pub. L. 111–203, title X, §1085(4), July 21, 2010, 124 Stat. 2084.)

EDITORIAL NOTES

REFERENCES IN TEXT

The Consumer Financial Protection Act of 2010, referred to in subsecs. (a) and (c), is title X of Pub. L. 111–203, July 21, 2010, 124 Stat. 1955. Subtitles B (§§1021–1029A) and E (§§1051–1058) of the Act are classified generally to parts B (§5511 et seq.) and E (§5561 et seq.), respectively, of subchapter V of chapter 53 of Title 12, Banks and Banking. For complete classification of subtitles B and E to the Code, see Tables.

Sections 25 and 25A of the Federal Reserve Act, referred to in subsec. (a)(1)(B), are classified to subchapters I (§601 et seq.) and II (§611 et seq.), respectively, of chapter 6 of Title 12, Banks and Banking.

The Federal Credit Union Act, referred to in subsec. (a)(2), is act June 26, 1934, ch. 750, 48 Stat. 1216, which is classified generally to chapter 14 (§1751 et seq.) of Title 12. For complete classification of this Act to the Code, see section 1751 of Title 12 and Tables.

The Packers and Stockyards Act, 1921, referred to in subsec. (a)(5), is act Aug. 15, 1921, ch. 64, 42 Stat. 159, which is classified to chapter 9 (§181 et seq.) of Title 7, Agriculture. For complete classification of this Act to the Code, see section 181 of Title 7 and Tables.

The Farm Credit Act of 1971, referred to in subsec. (a)(6), is Pub. L. 92–181, Dec. 10, 1971, 85 Stat. 583, which is classified generally to chapter 23 (§2001 et seq.) of Title 12, Banks and Banking. For complete classification of this Act to the Code, see Short Title note set out under section 2001 of Title 12 and Tables.

The Securities Exchange Act of 1934, referred to in subsec. (a)(7), is act June 6, 1934, ch. 404, 48 Stat. 881, which is classified principally to chapter 2B (§78a et seq.) of this title. For complete classification of this Act to the Code, see Codification note set out under section 78a of this title and Tables.

The Small Business Investment Act of 1958, referred to in subsec. (a)(8), is Pub. L. 85–699, Aug. 21, 1958, 72 Stat. 689, which is classified principally to chapter 14B (§661 et seq.) of this title. For complete classification of this Act to the Code, see Short Title note set out under section 661 of this title and Tables.

The Federal Trade Commission Act, referred to in subsec. (c), is act Sept. 26, 1914, ch. 311, 38 Stat. 717, which is classified generally to subchapter I (§41 et seq.) of chapter 2 of this title. For complete classification of this Act to the Code, see section 58 of this title and Tables.

This subchapter, referred to in subsec. (c) before "shall be deemed", probably should have been a reference to this title in the original, meaning title VII of Pub. L. 90–321 which is classified generally to this subchapter.

CODIFICATION

In subsec. (a)(3), "Subtitle IV of title 49" substituted for "The Acts to regulate commerce" on authority of Pub. L. 95–473, §3(b), Oct. 17, 1978, 92 Stat. 1466, the first section of which enacted subtitle IV of Title 49, Transportation.

In subsec. (a)(4), "Part A of subtitle VII of title 49" substituted for "The Federal Aviation Act of 1958 [49 App. U.S.C. 1301 et seq.]" and "that part" substituted for "that Act" on authority of Pub. L. 103–272, §6(b), July 5, 1994, 108 Stat. 1378, the first section of which enacted subtitles II, III, and V to X of Title 49.

AMENDMENTS

2010—Subsec. (a). Pub. L. 111–203, §1085(4)(A)(i), substituted "Subject to subtitle B of the Consumer Protection Financial Protection Act of 2010" for "Compliance" in introductory provisions.

Subsec. (a)(1). Pub. L. 111–203, §1085(4)(A)(ii), added par. (1) and struck out former par. (1) which read as follows: "section 8 of the Federal Deposit Insurance Act, in the case of—

"(A) national banks, and Federal branches and Federal agencies of foreign banks, by the Office of the Comptroller of the Currency;

"(B) member banks of the Federal Reserve System (other than national banks), branches and agencies of foreign banks (other than Federal branches, Federal agencies, and insured State branches of foreign banks), commercial lending companies owned or controlled by foreign banks, and organizations operating under section 25 or 25(a) of the Federal Reserve Act, by the Board; and

"(C) banks insured by the Federal Deposit Insurance Corporation (other than members of the Federal Reserve System) and insured State branches of foreign banks, by the Board of Directors of the Federal Deposit Insurance Corporation;".

Subsec. (a)(2) to (9). Pub. L. 111–203, §1085(4)(A)(ii)–(vi), added par. (9), redesignated former pars. (3) to (9) as (2) to (8), respectively, and struck out former par. (2) which read as follows: "Section 8 of the Federal Deposit Insurance Act, by the Director of the Office of Thrift Supervision, in the case of a savings association the deposits of which are insured by the Federal Deposit Insurance Corporation."

Subsec. (c). Pub. L. 111–203, §1085(4)(B), added subsec. (c) and struck out former subsec. (c) which read as follows: "Except to the extent that enforcement of the requirements imposed under this subchapter is specifically committed to some other Government agency under subsection (a) of this section, the Federal Trade Commission shall enforce such requirements. For the purpose of the exercise by the Federal Trade Commission of its functions and powers under the Federal Trade Commission Act, a violation of any requirement imposed under this subchapter shall be deemed a violation of a requirement imposed under that Act. All of the functions and powers of the Federal Trade Commission under the Federal Trade Commission Act are available to the Commission to enforce compliance by any person with the requirements imposed under this subchapter, irrespective of whether that person is engaged in commerce or meets any other jurisdictional tests in the Federal Trade Commission Act, including the power to enforce any Federal Reserve Board regulation promulgated under this subchapter in the same manner as if the violation had been a violation of a Federal Trade Commission trade regulation rule."

Subsec. (d). Pub. L. 111–203, §1085(4)(C), substituted "Bureau" for "Board".

1995—Subsec. (a)(4). Pub. L. 104–88 substituted "Secretary of Transportation, with respect to all carriers subject to the jurisdiction of the Surface Transportation Board" for "Interstate Commerce Commission with respect to any common carrier subject to those Acts".

1992—Subsec. (a)(1)(C). Pub. L. 102–550 substituted semicolon for period at end.

1991—Subsec. (a). Pub. L. 102–242, §212(d)(2), inserted at end "The terms used in paragraph (1) that are not defined in this subchapter or otherwise defined in section 3(s) of the Federal Deposit Insurance Act (12 U.S.C. 1813(s)) shall have the meaning given to them in section 1(b) of the International Banking Act of 1978 (12 U.S.C. 3101)."

Pub. L. 102–242, §212(d)(1), added par. (1) and struck out former par. (1) which read as follows: "Section 8 of Federal Deposit Insurance Act, in the case of—

"(A) national banks, by the Comptroller of the Currency,

"(B) member banks of the Federal Reserve System (other than national banks), by the Federal Reserve Board,

"(C) banks the deposits or accounts of which are insured by the Federal Deposit Insurance Corporation (other than members of the Federal Reserve System), by the Board of Directors of the Federal Deposit Insurance Corporation."

1989—Subsec. (a)(2). Pub. L. 101–73 amended par. (2) generally. Prior to amendment, par. (2) read as follows: "Section 5(d) of the Home Owners' Loan Act of 1933, section 407 of the National Housing Act, and sections 6(i) and 17 of the Federal Home Loan Bank Act, by the Federal Home Loan Bank Board (acting directly or through the Federal Savings and Loan Insurance Corporation), in the case of any institution subject to any of those provisions."

1984—Subsec. (a)(5). Pub. L. 98–443 substituted "Secretary of Transportation" for "Civil Aeronautics Board".

1976—Subsec. (c). Pub. L. 94–239 inserted provisions giving the Federal Trade Commission power to enforce any regulation of the Federal Reserve Board promulgated under this subchapter.

STATUTORY NOTES AND RELATED SUBSIDIARIES

EFFECTIVE DATE OF 2010 AMENDMENT

Amendment by Pub. L. 111–203 effective on the designated transfer date, see section 1100H of Pub. L. 111–203, set out as a note under section 552a of Title 5, Government Organization and Employees.

EFFECTIVE DATE OF 1995 AMENDMENT

Amendment by Pub. L. 104–88 effective Jan. 1, 1996, see section 2 of Pub. L. 104–88, set out as an Effective Date note under section 1301 of Title 49, Transportation.

EFFECTIVE DATE OF 1992 AMENDMENT

Amendment by Pub. L. 102–550 effective as if included in the Federal Deposit Insurance Corporation Improvement Act of 1991, Pub. L. 102–242, as of Dec. 19, 1991, see section 1609(a) of Pub. L. 102–550, set out as a note under section 191 of Title 12, Banks and Banking.

EFFECTIVE DATE OF 1984 AMENDMENT

Amendment by Pub. L. 98–443 effective Jan. 1, 1985, see section 9(v) of Pub. L. 98–443, set out as a note under section 5314 of Title 5, Government Organization and Employees.

EFFECTIVE DATE OF 1976 AMENDMENT

Amendment by Pub. L. 94–239 effective Mar. 23, 1976, see section 708 of Pub. L. 90–321, set out as an Effective Date note under section 1691 of this title.

TRANSFER OF FUNCTIONS

Functions vested in Administrator of National Credit Union Administration transferred and vested in National Credit Union Administration Board pursuant to section 1752a of Title 12, Banks and Banking.

[1] So in original. Probably should be "Consumer Financial Protection Act of 2010".

[2] So in original. Probably should be ", compliance with".

[3] See References in Text note below.

§1691c–1. Incentives for self-testing and self-correction

(a) Privileged information

(1) Conditions for privilege

A report or result of a self-test (as that term is defined by regulations of the Bureau) shall be considered to be privileged under paragraph (2) if a creditor—

(A) conducts, or authorizes an independent third party to conduct, a self-test of any aspect of a credit transaction by a creditor, in order to determine the level or effectiveness of compliance with this subchapter by the creditor; and

(B) has identified any possible violation of this subchapter by the creditor and has taken, or is taking, appropriate corrective action to address any such possible violation.

(2) Privileged self-test

If a creditor meets the conditions specified in subparagraphs (A) and (B) of paragraph (1) with respect to a self-test described in that paragraph, any report or results of that self-test—

(A) shall be privileged; and

(B) may not be obtained or used by any applicant, department, or agency in any—

(i) proceeding or civil action in which one or more violations of this subchapter are alleged; or

(ii) examination or investigation relating to compliance with this subchapter.

(b) Results of self-testing

(1) In general

No provision of this section may be construed to prevent an applicant, department, or agency from obtaining or using a report or results of any self-test in any proceeding or civil action in which a violation of this subchapter is alleged, or in any examination or investigation of compliance with this subchapter if—

(A) the creditor or any person with lawful access to the report or results—

(i) voluntarily releases or discloses all, or any part of, the report or results to the applicant, department, or agency, or to the general public; or

(ii) refers to or describes the report or results as a defense to charges of violations of this subchapter against the creditor to whom the self-test relates; or

(B) the report or results are sought in conjunction with an adjudication or admission of a violation of this subchapter for the sole purpose of determining an appropriate penalty or remedy.

(2) Disclosure for determination of penalty or remedy

Any report or results of a self-test that are disclosed for the purpose specified in paragraph (1)(B)—

(A) shall be used only for the particular proceeding in which the adjudication or admission referred to in paragraph (1)(B) is made; and

(B) may not be used in any other action or proceeding.

(c) Adjudication

An applicant, department, or agency that challenges a privilege asserted under this section may seek a determination of the existence and application of that privilege in—

(1) a court of competent jurisdiction; or

(2) an administrative law proceeding with appropriate jurisdiction.

(Pub. L. 90–321, title VII, §704A, as added Pub. L. 104–208, div. A, title II, §2302(a)(1), Sept. 30, 1996, 110 Stat. 3009–420; amended Pub. L. 111–203, title X, §1085(1), July 21, 2010, 124 Stat. 2083.)

EDITORIAL NOTES

AMENDMENTS

2010—Subsec. (a)(1). Pub. L. 111–203 substituted "Bureau" for "Board" in introductory provisions.

EFFECTIVE DATE OF 2010 AMENDMENT

Amendment by Pub. L. 111–203 effective on the designated transfer date, see section 1100H of Pub. L. 111–203, set out as a note under section 552a of Title 5, Government Organization and Employees.

EFFECTIVE DATE

Pub. L. 104–208, div. A, title III, §2302(c), Sept. 30, 1996, 110 Stat. 3009–423, provided that:

"(1) IN GENERAL.—Except as provided in paragraph (2), the privilege provided for in section 704A of the Equal Credit Opportunity Act [15 U.S.C. 1691c–1] or section 814A of the Fair Housing Act [42 U.S.C. 3614–1] (as those sections are added by this section) shall apply to a self-test (as that term is defined pursuant to the regulations prescribed under subsection (a)(2) [set out below] or (b)(2) of this section [42 U.S.C. 3614–1 note], as appropriate) conducted before, on, or after the effective date of the regulations prescribed under subsection (a)(2) or (b)(2), as appropriate.

"(2) EXCEPTION.—The privilege referred to in paragraph (1) does not apply to such a self-test conducted before the effective date of the regulations prescribed under subsection (a) or (b), as appropriate, if—

"(A) before that effective date, a complaint against the creditor or person engaged in residential real estate related lending activities (as the case may be) was—

"(i) formally filed in any court of competent jurisdiction; or

"(ii) the subject of an ongoing administrative law proceeding;

"(B) in the case of section 704A of the Equal Credit Opportunity Act, the creditor has waived the privilege pursuant to subsection (b)(1)(A)(i) of that section; or

"(C) in the case of section 814A of the Fair Housing Act, the person engaged in residential real estate related lending activities has waived the privilege pursuant to subsection (b)(1)(A)(i) of that section."

REGULATIONS

Pub. L. 104–208, div. A, title III, §2302(a)(2), Sept. 30, 1996, 110 Stat. 3009–421, provided that:

"(A) IN GENERAL.—Not later than 6 months after the date of enactment of this Act [Sept. 30, 1996], in consultation with the Secretary of Housing and Urban Development and the agencies referred to in section 704 of the Equal Credit Opportunity Act [15 U.S.C. 1691c], and after providing notice and an opportunity for public comment, the Board shall prescribe final regulations to implement section 704A of the Equal Credit Opportunity Act [15 U.S.C. 1691c–1], as added by this section.

"(B) SELF-TEST.—

"(i) DEFINITION.—The regulations prescribed under subparagraph (A) shall include a definition of the term 'self-test' for purposes of section 704A of the Equal Credit Opportunity Act, as added by this section.

"(ii) REQUIREMENT FOR SELF-TEST.—The regulations prescribed under subparagraph (A) shall specify that a self-test shall be sufficiently extensive to constitute a determination of the level and effectiveness of compliance by a creditor with the Equal Credit Opportunity Act [15 U.S.C. 1691 et seq.].

"(iii) SUBSTANTIAL SIMILARITY TO CERTAIN FAIR HOUSING ACT REGULATIONS.—The regulations prescribed under subparagraph (A) shall be substantially similar to the regulations prescribed by the Secretary of Housing and Urban Development to carry out section 814A(d) of the Fair Housing Act [42 U.S.C. 3614–1(d)], as added by this section."

§1691c–2. Small business loan data collection

(a) Purpose

The purpose of this section is to facilitate enforcement of fair lending laws and enable communities, governmental entities, and creditors to identify business and community development needs and opportunities of women-owned, minority-owned, and small businesses.

(b) Information gathering

Subject to the requirements of this section, in the case of any application to a financial institution for credit for women-owned, minority-owned, or small business, the financial institution shall—

(1) inquire whether the business is a women-owned, minority-owned, or small business, without regard to whether such application is received in person, by mail, by telephone, by electronic mail or other form of electronic transmission, or by any other means, and whether or not such application is in response to a solicitation by the financial institution; and

(2) maintain a record of the responses to such inquiry, separate from the application and accompanying information.

(c) Right to refuse

Any applicant for credit may refuse to provide any information requested pursuant to subsection (b) in connection with any application for credit.

(d) No access by underwriters

(1) Limitation

Where feasible, no loan underwriter or other officer or employee of a financial institution, or any affiliate of a financial institution, involved in making any determination concerning an application for credit shall have access to any information provided by the applicant pursuant to a request under subsection (b) in connection with such application.

(2) Limited access

If a financial institution determines that a loan underwriter or other officer or employee of a financial institution, or any affiliate of a financial institution, involved in making any determination concerning an application for credit should have access to any information provided by the applicant pursuant to a request under subsection (b), the financial institution shall provide notice to the applicant of the access of the underwriter to such information, along with notice that the financial institution may not discriminate on the basis of such information.

(e) Form and manner of information

(1) In general

Each financial institution shall compile and maintain, in accordance with regulations of the Bureau, a record of the information provided by any loan applicant pursuant to a request under subsection (b).

(2) Itemization

Information compiled and maintained under paragraph (1) shall be itemized in order to clearly and conspicuously disclose—

(A) the number of the application and the date on which the application was received;

(B) the type and purpose of the loan or other credit being applied for;

(C) the amount of the credit or credit limit applied for, and the amount of the credit transaction or the credit limit approved for such applicant;

(D) the type of action taken with respect to such application, and the date of such action;

(E) the census tract in which is located the principal place of business of the women-owned, minority-owned, or small business loan applicant;

(F) the gross annual revenue of the business in the last fiscal year of the women-owned, minority-owned, or small business loan applicant preceding the date of the application;

(G) the race, sex, and ethnicity of the principal owners of the business; and

(H) any additional data that the Bureau determines would aid in fulfilling the purposes of this section.

(3) No personally identifiable information

In compiling and maintaining any record of information under this section, a financial institution may not include in such record the name, specific address (other than the census tract required under paragraph (1)(E)),[1] telephone number, electronic mail address, or any other personally identifiable information concerning any individual who is, or is connected with, the women-owned, minority-owned, or small business loan applicant.

(4) Discretion to delete or modify publicly available data

The Bureau may, at its discretion, delete or modify data collected under this section which is or will be available to the public, if the Bureau determines that the deletion or modification of the data would advance a privacy interest.

(f) Availability of information

(1) Submission to Bureau

The data required to be compiled and maintained under this section by any financial institution shall be submitted annually to the Bureau.

(2) Availability of information

Information compiled and maintained under this section shall be—

(A) retained for not less than 3 years after the date of preparation;

(B) made available to any member of the public, upon request, in the form required under regulations prescribed by the Bureau;

(C) annually made available to the public generally by the Bureau, in such form and in such manner as is determined by the Bureau, by regulation.

(3) Compilation of aggregate data

The Bureau may, at its discretion—

(A) compile and aggregate data collected under this section for its own use; and

(B) make public such compilations of aggregate data.

(g) Bureau action

(1) In general

The Bureau shall prescribe such rules and issue such guidance as may be necessary to carry out, enforce, and compile data pursuant to this section.

(2) Exceptions

The Bureau, by rule or order, may adopt exceptions to any requirement of this section and may, conditionally or unconditionally, exempt any financial institution or class of financial institutions from the requirements of this section, as the Bureau deems necessary or appropriate to carry out the purposes of this section.

(3) Guidance

The Bureau shall issue guidance designed to facilitate compliance with the requirements of this section, including assisting financial institutions in working with applicants to determine whether the applicants are women-owned, minority-owned, or small businesses for purposes of this section.

(h) Definitions

For purposes of this section, the following definitions shall apply:

(1) Financial institution

The term "financial institution" means any partnership, company, corporation, association (incorporated or unincorporated), trust, estate, cooperative organization, or other entity that engages in any financial activity.

(2) Small business

The term "small business" has the same meaning as the term "small business concern" in section 632 of this title.

(3) Small business loan

The term "small business loan" means a loan made to a small business.

(4) Minority

The term "minority" has the same meaning as in section 1204(c)(3) of the Financial Institutions Reform, Recovery, and Enforcement Act of 1989.

(5) Minority-owned business

The term "minority-owned business" means a business—

(A) more than 50 percent of the ownership or control of which is held by 1 or more minority individuals; and

(B) more than 50 percent of the net profit or loss of which accrues to 1 or more minority individuals.

(6) Women-owned business

The term "women-owned business" means a business—

(A) more than 50 percent of the ownership or control of which is held by 1 or more women; and

(B) more than 50 percent of the net profit or loss of which accrues to 1 or more women.

(Pub. L. 90–321, title VII, §704B, as added Pub. L. 111–203, title X, §1071(a), July 21, 2010, 124 Stat. 2056.)

EDITORIAL NOTES

REFERENCES IN TEXT

Section 1204(c)(3) of the Financial Institutions Reform, Recovery, and Enforcement Act of 1989, referred to in subsec. (h)(4), is section 1204(c)(3) of Pub. L. 101–73, which is set out as a note under section 1811 of Title 12, Banks and Banking.

STATUTORY NOTES AND RELATED SUBSIDIARIES

EFFECTIVE DATE

Section effective on the designated transfer date, see section 1071(d) of Pub. L. 111–203, set out as an Effective Date of 2010 Amendment note under section 1691 of this title.

¹ So in original. Probably should be "721(E)."

§1691d. Applicability of other laws

(a) Requests for signature of husband and wife for creation of valid lien, etc.

A request for the signature of both parties to a marriage for the purpose of creating a valid lien, passing clear title, waiving inchoate rights to property, or assigning earnings, shall not constitute discrimination under this subchapter: Provided, however, That this provision shall not be construed to permit a creditor to take sex or marital status into account in connection with the evaluation of creditworthiness of any applicant.

(b) State property laws affecting creditworthiness

Consideration or application of State property laws directly or indirectly affecting creditworthiness shall not constitute discrimination for purposes of this subchapter.

(c) State laws prohibiting separate extension of consumer credit to husband and wife

Any provision of State law which prohibits the separate extension of consumer credit to each party to a marriage shall not apply in any case where each party to a marriage voluntarily applies for separate credit from the same creditor: Provided, That in any case where such a State law is so preempted, each party to the marriage shall be solely responsible for the debt so contracted.

(d) Combining credit accounts of husband and wife with same creditor to determine permissible finance charges or loan ceilings under Federal or State laws

When each party to a marriage separately and voluntarily applies for and obtains separate credit accounts with the same creditor, those accounts shall not be aggregated or otherwise combined for purposes of determining permissible finance charges or permissible loan ceilings under the laws of any State or of the United States.

(e) Election of remedies under subchapter or State law; nature of relief determining applicability

Where the same act or omission constitutes a violation of this subchapter and of applicable State law, a person aggrieved by such conduct may bring a legal action to recover monetary damages either under this subchapter or under such State law, but not both. This election of remedies shall not apply to court actions in which the relief sought does not include monetary damages or to administrative actions.

(f) Compliance with inconsistent State laws; determination of inconsistency

This subchapter does not annul, alter, or affect, or exempt any person subject to the provisions of this subchapter from complying with, the laws of any State with respect to credit discrimination, except to the extent that those laws are inconsistent with any provision of this subchapter, and then only to the extent of the inconsistency. The Bureau is authorized to determine whether such inconsistencies exist. The Bureau may not determine that any State law is inconsistent with any provision of this subchapter if the Bureau determines that such law gives greater protection to the applicant.

(g) Exemption by regulation of credit transactions covered by State law; failure to comply with State law

The Bureau shall by regulation exempt from the requirements of sections 1691 and 1691a of this title any class of credit transactions within any State if it determines that under the law of that State that class of transactions is subject to requirements substantially similar to those imposed under this subchapter or that such law gives greater protection to the applicant, and that there is adequate provision for enforcement. Failure to comply with any requirement of such State law in any transaction so exempted shall constitute a violation of this subchapter for the purposes of section 1691e of this title.

(Pub. L. 90–321, title VII, §705, as added Pub. L. 93–495, title V, §503, Oct. 28, 1974, 88 Stat. 1523; amended Pub. L. 94–239, §5, Mar. 23, 1976, 90 Stat. 253; Pub. L. 111–203, title X, §1085(1), July 21, 2010, 124 Stat. 2083.)

Editorial Notes

Amendments

2010—Subsecs. (f), (g). Pub. L. 111–203 substituted "Bureau" for "Board" wherever appearing.

1976—Subsec. (e). Pub. L. 94–239, §5(1), substituted provisions requiring an election of remedies in legal actions involving the recovery of monetary damages, for provisions specifying a general election of remedies.

Subsecs. (f), (g). Pub. L. 94–239, §5(2), added subsecs. (f) and (g).

Statutory Notes and Related Subsidiaries

Effective Date of 2010 Amendment

Amendment by Pub. L. 111–203 effective on the designated transfer date, see section 1100H of Pub. L. 111–203, set out as a note under section 552a of Title 5, Government Organization and Employees.

Effective Date of 1976 Amendment

Amendment by Pub. L. 94–239 effective Mar. 23, 1976, see section 708 of Pub. L. 90–321, set out as an Effective Date note under section 1691 of this title.

§1691e. Civil liability

(a) Individual or class action for actual damages

Any creditor who fails to comply with any requirement imposed under this subchapter shall be liable to the aggrieved applicant for any actual damages sustained by such applicant acting either in an individual capacity or as a member of a class.

(b) Recovery of punitive damages in individual and class action for actual damages; exemptions; maximum amount of punitive damages in individual actions; limitation on total recovery in class actions; factors determining amount of award

Any creditor, other than a government or governmental subdivision or agency, who fails to comply with any requirement imposed under this subchapter shall be liable to the aggrieved applicant for punitive damages in an amount not greater than $10,000, in addition to any actual damages provided in subsection (a), except that in the case of a class action the total recovery under this subsection shall not exceed the lesser of $500,000 or 1 per centum of the net worth of the creditor. In determining the amount of such damages in any action, the court shall consider, among other relevant factors, the amount of any actual damages awarded, the frequency and persistence of failures of compliance by the creditor, the resources of the creditor, the number of persons adversely affected, and the extent to which the creditor's failure of compliance was intentional.

(c) Action for equitable and declaratory relief

Upon application by an aggrieved applicant, the appropriate United States district court or any other court of competent jurisdiction may grant such equitable and declaratory relief as is necessary to enforce the requirements imposed under this subchapter.

(d) Recovery of costs and attorney fees

In the case of any successful action under subsection (a), (b), or (c), the costs of the action, together with a reasonable attorney's fee as determined by the court, shall be added to any damages awarded by the court under such subsection.

(e) Good faith compliance with rule, regulation, or interpretation of Bureau or interpretation or approval by an official or employee of Bureau of Consumer Financial Protection duly authorized by Bureau

No provision of this subchapter imposing liability shall apply to any act done or omitted in good faith in conformity with any official rule, regulation, or interpretation thereof by the Bureau or in conformity with any interpretation or approval by an official or employee of the Bureau of Consumer Financial Protection duly authorized by the Bureau to issue such interpretations or approvals under such procedures as the Bureau may prescribe therefor, notwithstanding that after such act or omission has occurred, such rule, regulation, interpretation, or approval is amended, rescinded, or determined by judicial or other authority to be invalid for any reason.

(f) Jurisdiction of courts; time for maintenance of action; exceptions

Any action under this section may be brought in the appropriate United States district court without regard to the amount in controversy, or in any other court of competent jurisdiction. No such action shall be brought later than 5 years after the date of the occurrence of the violation, except that—

(1) whenever any agency having responsibility for administrative enforcement under section 1691c of this title commences an enforcement proceeding within 5 years after the date of the occurrence of the violation,

(2) whenever the Attorney General commences a civil action under this section within 5 years after the date of the occurrence of the violation,

then any applicant who has been a victim of the discrimination which is the subject of such proceeding or civil action may bring an action under this section not later than one year after the commencement of that proceeding or action.

(g) Request by responsible enforcement agency to Attorney General for civil action

The agencies having responsibility for administrative enforcement under section 1691c of this title, if unable to obtain compliance with section 1691 of this title, are authorized to refer the matter to the Attorney General with a recommendation that an appropriate civil action be instituted. Each agency referred to in paragraphs (1), (2), and (8) of section 1691c(a) of this title shall refer the matter to the Attorney General whenever the agency has reason to believe that 1 or more creditors has engaged in a pattern or practice of discouraging or denying applications for credit in violation of section 1691(a) of this title. Each such agency may refer the matter to the Attorney General whenever the agency has reason to believe that 1 or more creditors has violated section 1691(a) of this title.

(h) Authority for Attorney General to bring civil action; jurisdiction

When a matter is referred to the Attorney General pursuant to subsection (g), or whenever he has reason to believe that one or more creditors are engaged in a pattern or practice in violation of this subchapter, the Attorney General may bring a civil action in any appropriate United States district court for such relief as may be appropriate, including actual and punitive damages and injunctive relief.

(i) Recovery under both subchapter and fair housing enforcement provisions prohibited for violation based on same transaction

No person aggrieved by a violation of this subchapter and by a violation of section 3605 of title 42 shall recover under this subchapter and section 3612 [1] of title 42, if such violation is based on the same transaction.

(j) Discovery of creditor's granting standards

Nothing in this subchapter shall be construed to prohibit the discovery of a creditor's credit granting standards under appropriate discovery procedures in the court or agency in which an action or proceeding is brought.

(k) Notice to HUD of violations

Whenever an agency referred to in paragraph (1), (2), or (3) [1] of section 1691c(a) of this title—

(1) has reason to believe, as a result of receiving a consumer complaint, conducting a consumer compliance examination, or otherwise, that a violation of this subchapter has occurred;

(2) has reason to believe that the alleged violation would be a violation of the Fair Housing Act [42 U.S.C. 3601 et seq.]; and

(3) does not refer the matter to the Attorney General pursuant to subsection (g),

the agency shall notify the Secretary of Housing and Urban Development of the violation, and shall notify the applicant that the Secretary of Housing and Urban Development has been notified of the alleged violation and that remedies for the violation may be available under the Fair Housing Act.

(Pub. L. 90–321, title VII, §706, as added Pub. L. 93–495, title V, §503, Oct. 28, 1974, 88 Stat. 1524; amended Pub. L. 94–239, §8, Mar. 23, 1976, 90 Stat. 253; Pub. L. 102–242, title II, §223(a)–(c), Dec. 19, 1991, 105 Stat. 2306; Pub. L. 111–203, title X, §1085(1), (5)–(7), July 21, 2010, 124 Stat. 2083, 2085.)

EDITORIAL NOTES

REFERENCES IN TEXT

Section 3612 of title 42, referred to in subsec. (i), which related to enforcement of the Fair Housing Act (42 U.S.C. 3601 et seq.) by private persons, was repealed by Pub. L. 100–430, §8(2), Sept. 13, 1988, 102 Stat. 1625. See section 3613 of Title 42, The Public Health and Welfare.

Paragraph (1), (2), or (3) of section 1691c(a) of this title, referred to in subsec. (k), probably means par. (1), (2), or (3) of section 1691c(a) of this title prior to repeal of pars. (1) and (2), enactment of new pars. (1) and (9), and redesignation of par. (3) as (2) by Pub. L. 111–203, title X, §1085(4)(A)(iii)–(vi), July 21, 2010, 124 Stat. 2084.

The Fair Housing Act, referred to in subsec. (k), is title VIII of Pub. L. 90–284, Apr. 11, 1968, 82 Stat. 81, which is classified principally to subchapter I (§3601 et seq.) of chapter 45 of Title 42. For complete classification of this Act to the Code, see Short Title note set out under section 3601 of Title 42 and Tables.

AMENDMENTS

2010—Subsec. (e). Pub. L. 111–203, §1085(5)(B), substituted "Bureau of Consumer Financial Protection" for "Federal Reserve System" in text.

Pub. L. 111–203, §1085(5)(A), which directed amendment of "subsection heading" by substituting "Bureau" for "Board" wherever appearing and "Bureau of Consumer Financial Protection" for "Federal Reserve System", was executed by making the substitutions in heading that had been supplied editorially, to reflect the probable intent of Congress.

Pub. L. 111–203, §1085(1), substituted "Bureau" for "Board" wherever appearing.

Subsec. (f). Pub. L. 111–203, §1085(7), substituted "5 years after" for "two years from" wherever appearing.

Subsec. (g). Pub. L. 111–203, §1085(6), substituted "(9)" for "(3)".

1991—Subsec. (g). Pub. L. 102–242, §223(a), inserted at end "Each agency referred to in paragraphs (1), (2), and (3) of section 1691c(a) of this title shall refer the matter to the Attorney General whenever the agency has reason to believe that 1 or more creditors has engaged in a pattern or practice of discouraging or denying applications for credit in violation of section 1691(a) of this title. Each such agency may refer the matter to the Attorney General whenever the agency has reason to believe that 1 or more creditors has violated section 1691(a) of this title."

Subsec. (h). Pub. L. 102–242, §223(b), inserted "actual and punitive damages and" after "be appropriate, including".

Subsec. (k). Pub. L. 102–242, §223(c), added subsec. (k).

1976—Subsec. (a). Pub. L. 94–239 substituted reference to member for reference to representative.

Subsec. (b). Pub. L. 94–239 inserted provisions exempting government or governmental subdivision or agency from requirements of this subchapter, incorporated provisions contained in former subsec. (c) relating to recovery in class actions and, as incorporated, raised the total amount of recovery under a class action from $100,000 to $500,000.

Subsec. (c). Pub. L. 94–239 redesignated subsec. (d) as (c) and specified United States district court or other court of competent jurisdiction as court in which to bring action, and substituted provisions authorizing such court to grant equitable and declaratory relief, for provisions authorizing civil actions for preventive relief. Provisions of former subsec. (c) were incorporated into present subsec. (b) and amended.

Subsec. (d). Pub. L. 94–239 redesignated subsec. (e) as (d) and made minor changes in phraseology. Former subsec. (d) redesignated (c) and amended.

Subsec. (e). Pub. L. 94–239 redesignated subsec. (f) as (e) and inserted reference to officially promulgated rule, regulation, or interpretation and provisions relating to approval and interpretations by an official or employee of the Federal Reserve System duly authorized by the Board. Former subsec. (e) redesignated (d) and amended.

Subsec. (f). Pub. L. 94–239 redesignated subsec. (g) as (f) and inserted provisions which substituted a two-year limitation for one year limitation and provisions extending time in which to bring action under enumerated conditions. Former subsec. (f) redesignated (e) and amended.

Subsecs. (g) to (j). Pub. L. 94–239 added subsecs. (g) to (j). Former subsec. (g) redesignated (f) and amended.

STATUTORY NOTES AND RELATED SUBSIDIARIES

EFFECTIVE DATE OF 2010 AMENDMENT

Amendment by Pub. L. 111–203 effective on the designated transfer date, see section 1100H of Pub. L. 111–203, set out as a note under section 552a of Title 5, Government Organization and Employees.

EFFECTIVE DATE OF 1976 AMENDMENT

Amendment by Pub. L. 94–239 effective Mar. 23, 1976, see section 708 of Pub. L. 90–321, set out as an Effective Date note under section 1691 of this title.

† See References in Text note below.

§1691f. Annual reports to Congress; contents

Each year, the Bureau and the Attorney General shall, respectively, make reports to the Congress concerning the administration of their functions under this subchapter, including such recommendations as the Bureau and the Attorney General, respectively, deem necessary or appropriate. In addition, each report of the Bureau shall include its assessment of the extent to which compliance with the requirements of this subchapter is being achieved, and a summary of the enforcement actions taken by each of the agencies assigned administrative enforcement responsibilities under section 1691c of this title.

(Pub. L. 90–321, title VII, §707, as added Pub. L. 94–239, §7, Mar. 23, 1976, 90 Stat. 255; amended Pub. L. 96–221, title VI, §610(c), Mar. 31, 1980, 94 Stat. 174; Pub. L. 111–203, title X, §1085(1), July 21, 2010, 124 Stat. 2083.)

EDITORIAL NOTES

AMENDMENTS

2010—Pub. L. 111–203 substituted "Bureau" for "Board" wherever appearing.
1980—Pub. L. 96–221 substituted "Each year" for "Not later than February 1 of each year after 1976".

STATUTORY NOTES AND RELATED SUBSIDIARIES

EFFECTIVE DATE OF 2010 AMENDMENT

Amendment by Pub. L. 111–203 effective on the designated transfer date, see section 1100H of Pub. L. 111–203, set out as a note under section 552a of Title 5, Government Organization and Employees.

Effective Date of 1980 Amendment

Amendment by Pub. L. 96–221 effective on expiration of two years and six months after Mar. 31, 1980, with all regulations, forms, and clauses required to be prescribed to be promulgated at least one year prior to such effective date, and allowing any creditor to comply with any amendments, in accordance with the regulations, forms, and clauses prescribed by the Board prior to such effective date, see section 625 of Pub. L. 96–221, set out as a note under section 1602 of this file.

Effective Date

Section effective Mar. 23, 1976, see section 708 of Pub. L. 90–321, set out as a note under section 1691 of this file.

This marks the end of the Equal Credit opportunity Act
15 U.S.C. §§ 1691-1691f

FAIR DEBT COLLECTION PRACTICES ACT

15 U.S.C. §§ 1692-1692p, as amended

The FTC enforces the Fair Debt Collection Practices Act ("FDCPA"), which prohibits deceptive, unfair, and abusive debt collection practices. Among other things, the FDCPA bars collectors from using obscene or profane language, threatening violence, calling consumers repeatedly or at unreasonable hours, misrepresenting a consumer's legal rights, disclosing a consumer's personal affairs to third parties, and obtaining information about a consumer through false pretenses. Because certain practices that violate the FDCPA also violate the FTC Act, the FTC also uses the FTC Act to halt unfair or deceptive debt collection practices.

Revised January 2024

SUBCHAPTER V—DEBT COLLECTION PRACTICES

§1692. Congressional findings and declaration of purpose

(a) Abusive practices

There is abundant evidence of the use of abusive, deceptive, and unfair debt collection practices by many debt collectors. Abusive debt collection practices contribute to the number of personal bankruptcies, to marital instability, to the loss of jobs, and to invasions of individual privacy.

(b) Inadequacy of laws

Existing laws and procedures for redressing these injuries are inadequate to protect consumers.

(c) Available non-abusive collection methods

Means other than misrepresentation or other abusive debt collection practices are available for the effective collection of debts.

(d) Interstate commerce

Abusive debt collection practices are carried on to a substantial extent in interstate commerce and through means and instrumentalities of such commerce. Even where abusive debt collection practices are purely intrastate in character, they nevertheless directly affect interstate commerce.

(e) Purposes

It is the purpose of this subchapter to eliminate abusive debt collection practices by debt collectors, to insure that those debt collectors who refrain from using abusive debt collection practices are not competitively disadvantaged, and to promote consistent State action to protect consumers against debt collection abuses.

(Pub. L. 90–321, title VIII, §802, as added Pub. L. 95–109, Sept. 20, 1977, 91 Stat. 874.)

STATUTORY NOTES AND RELATED SUBSIDIARIES

EFFECTIVE DATE

Pub. L. 90–321, title VIII, §819, formerly §818, as added by Pub. L. 95–109, Sept. 20, 1977, 91 Stat. 883, §818; renumbered §819, Pub. L. 109–351, title VIII, §801(a)(1), Oct. 13, 2006, 120 Stat. 2004, provided that: "This title [enacting this subchapter] takes effect upon the expiration of six months after the date of its enactment [Sept. 20, 1977], but section 809 [section 1692g of this title] shall apply only with respect to debts for which the initial attempt to collect occurs after such effective date."

SHORT TITLE

This subchapter known as the "Fair Debt Collection Practices Act", see Short Title note set out under section 1601 of this title.

§1692a. Definitions

As used in this subchapter—

(1) The term "Bureau" means the Bureau of Consumer Financial Protection.

(2) The term "communication" means the conveying of information regarding a debt directly or indirectly to any person through any medium.

(3) The term "consumer" means any natural person obligated or allegedly obligated to pay any debt.

(4) The term "creditor" means any person who offers or extends credit creating a debt or to whom a debt is owed, but such term does not include any person to the extent that he receives an assignment or transfer of a debt in default solely for the purpose of facilitating collection of such debt for another.

(5) The term "debt" means any obligation or alleged obligation of a consumer to pay money arising out of a transaction in which the money, property, insurance, or services which are the subject of the transaction are primarily

for personal, family, or household purposes, whether or not such obligation has been reduced to judgment.

(6) The term "debt collector" means any person who uses any instrumentality of interstate commerce or the mails in any business the principal purpose of which is the collection of any debts, or who regularly collects or attempts to collect, directly or indirectly, debts owed or due or asserted to be owed or due another. Notwithstanding the exclusion provided by clause (F) of the last sentence of this paragraph, the term includes any creditor who, in the process of collecting his own debts, uses any name other than his own which would indicate that a third person is collecting or attempting to collect such debts. For the purpose of section 1692f(6) of this title, such term also includes any person who uses any instrumentality of interstate commerce or the mails in any business the principal purpose of which is the enforcement of security interests. The term does not include—

(A) any officer or employee of a creditor while, in the name of the creditor, collecting debts for such creditor;

(B) any person while acting as a debt collector for another person, both of whom are related by common ownership or affiliated by corporate control, if the person acting as a debt collector does so only for persons to whom it is so related or affiliated and if the principal business of such person is not the collection of debts;

(C) any officer or employee of the United States or any State to the extent that collecting or attempting to collect any debt is in the performance of his official duties;

(D) any person while serving or attempting to serve legal process on any other person in connection with the judicial enforcement of any debt;

(E) any nonprofit organization which, at the request of consumers, performs bona fide consumer credit counseling and assists consumers in the liquidation of their debts by receiving payments from such consumers and distributing such amounts to creditors; and

(F) any person collecting or attempting to collect any debt owed or due or asserted to be owed or due another to the extent such activity (i) is incidental to a bona fide fiduciary obligation or a bona fide escrow arrangement; (ii) concerns a debt which was originated by such person; (iii) concerns a debt which was not in default at the time it was obtained by such person; or (iv) concerns a debt obtained by such person as a secured party in a commercial credit transaction involving the creditor.

(7) The term "location information" means a consumer's place of abode and his telephone number at such place, or his place of employment.

(8) The term "State" means any State, territory, or possession of the United States, the District of Columbia, the Commonwealth of Puerto Rico, or any political subdivision of any of the foregoing.

(Pub. L. 90–321, title VIII, §803, as added Pub. L. 95–109, Sept. 20, 1977, 91 Stat. 875; amended Pub. L. 99–361, July 9, 1986, 100 Stat. 768; Pub. L. 111–203, title X, §1089(2), July 21, 2010, 124 Stat. 2092.)

EDITORIAL NOTES

AMENDMENTS

2010—Par. (1). Pub. L. 111–203 added par. (1) and struck out former par. (1) which read as follows: "The term 'Commission' means the Federal Trade Commission."

1986—Par. (6). Pub. L. 99–361 in provision preceding cl. (A) substituted "clause (F)" for "clause (G)", struck out cl. (F) which excluded any attorney-at-law collecting a debt as an attorney on behalf of and in the name of a client from term "debt collector", and redesignated cl. (G) as (F).

STATUTORY NOTES AND RELATED SUBSIDIARIES

EFFECTIVE DATE OF 2010 AMENDMENT

Amendment by Pub. L. 111–203 effective on the designated transfer date, see section 1100H of Pub. L. 111–203, set out as a note under section 552a of Title 5, Government Organization and Employees.

EFFECTIVE DATE

Section effective upon the expiration of six months after Sept. 20, 1977, see section 819 of Pub. L. 90–321, as added by Pub. L. 95–109, set out as a note under section 1692 of this title.

§1692b. Acquisition of location information

Any debt collector communicating with any person other than the consumer for the purpose of acquiring location information about the consumer shall—

(1) identify himself, state that he is confirming or correcting location information concerning the consumer, and, only if expressly requested, identify his employer;

(2) not state that such consumer owes any debt;

(3) not communicate with any such person more than once unless requested to do so by such person or unless the debt collector reasonably believes that the earlier response of such person is erroneous or incomplete and that such person now has correct or complete location information;

(4) not communicate by post card;

(5) not use any language or symbol on any envelope or in the contents of any communication effected by the mails or telegram that indicates that the debt collector is in the debt collection business or that the communication relates to the collection of a debt; and

(6) after the debt collector knows the consumer is represented by an attorney with regard to the subject debt and has knowledge of, or can readily ascertain, such attorney's name and address, not communicate with any person other than that attorney, unless the attorney fails to respond within a reasonable period of time to communication from the debt collector.

(Pub. L. 90–321, title VIII, §804, as added Pub. L. 95–109, Sept. 20, 1977, 91 Stat. 876.)

STATUTORY NOTES AND RELATED SUBSIDIARIES

EFFECTIVE DATE

Section effective upon the expiration of six months after Sept. 20, 1977, see section 819 of Pub. L. 90–321, as added by Pub. L. 95–109, set out as a note under section 1692 of this title.

§1692c. Communication in connection with debt collection

(a) Communication with the consumer generally

Without the prior consent of the consumer given directly to the debt collector or the express permission of a court of competent jurisdiction, a debt collector may not communicate with a consumer in connection with the collection of any debt—

(1) at any unusual time or place or a time or place known or which should be known to be inconvenient to the consumer. In the absence of knowledge of circumstances to the contrary, a debt collector shall assume that the convenient time for communicating with a consumer is after 8 o'clock antemeridian and before 9 o'clock postmeridian, local time at the consumer's location;

(2) if the debt collector knows the consumer is represented by an attorney with respect to such debt and has knowledge of, or can readily ascertain, such attorney's name and address, unless the attorney fails to respond within a reasonable period of time to a communication from the debt collector or unless the attorney consents to direct communication with the consumer; or

(3) at the consumer's place of employment if the debt collector knows or has reason to know that the consumer's employer prohibits the consumer from receiving such communication.

(b) Communication with third parties

Except as provided in section 1692b of this title, without the prior consent of the consumer given directly to the debt collector, or the express permission of a court of competent jurisdiction, or as reasonably necessary to effectuate a postjudgment judicial remedy, a debt collector may not communicate, in connection with the collection of any debt, with any person other than the consumer, his attorney, a consumer reporting agency if otherwise permitted by law, the creditor, the attorney of the creditor, or the attorney of the debt collector.

(c) Ceasing communication

If a consumer notifies a debt collector in writing that the consumer refuses to pay a debt or that the consumer wishes the debt collector to cease further communication with the consumer, the debt collector shall not communicate further with the consumer with respect to such debt, except—

(1) to advise the consumer that the debt collector's further efforts are being terminated;

(2) to notify the consumer that the debt collector or creditor may invoke specified remedies which are ordinarily invoked by such debt collector or creditor; or

(3) where applicable, to notify the consumer that the debt collector or creditor intends to invoke a specified remedy.

If such notice from the consumer is made by mail, notification shall be complete upon receipt.

(d) "Consumer" defined

For the purpose of this section, the term "consumer" includes the consumer's spouse, parent (if the consumer is a minor), guardian, executor, or administrator.

(Pub. L. 90–321, title VIII, §805, as added Pub. L. 95–109, Sept. 20, 1977, 91 Stat. 876.)

STATUTORY NOTES AND RELATED SUBSIDIARIES

Section effective upon the expiration of six months after Sept. 20, 1977, see section 819 of Pub. L. 90–321, as added by Pub. L. 95–109, set out as a note under section 1692 of this title.

§1692d. Harassment or abuse

A debt collector may not engage in any conduct the natural consequence of which is to harass, oppress, or abuse any person in connection with the collection of a debt. Without limiting the general application of the foregoing, the following conduct is a violation of this section:

(1) The use or threat of use of violence or other criminal means to harm the physical person, reputation, or property of any person.

(2) The use of obscene or profane language or language the natural consequence of which is to abuse the hearer or reader.

(3) The publication of a list of consumers who allegedly refuse to pay debts, except to a consumer reporting agency or to persons meeting the requirements of section 1681a(f) or 1681b(3) [1] of this title.

(4) The advertisement for sale of any debt to coerce payment of the debt.

(5) Causing a telephone to ring or engaging any person in telephone conversation repeatedly or continuously with intent to annoy, abuse, or harass any person at the called number.

(6) Except as provided in section 1692b of this title, the placement of telephone calls without meaningful disclosure of the caller's identity.

(Pub. L. 90–321, title VIII, §806, as added Pub. L. 95–109, Sept. 20, 1977, 91 Stat. 877.)

EDITORIAL NOTES

REFERENCES IN TEXT

Section 1681b(3) of this title, referred to in par. (3), was redesignated section 1681b(a)(3) of this title by Pub. L. 104–208, div. A, title II, §2403(a)(1), Sept. 30, 1996, 110 Stat. 3009–430.

STATUTORY NOTES AND RELATED SUBSIDIARIES

EFFECTIVE DATE

Section effective upon the expiration of six months after Sept. 20, 1977, see section 819 of Pub. L. 90–321, as added by Pub. L. 95–109, set out as a note under section 1692 of this title.

[1] *See References in Text note below.*

§1692e. False or misleading representations

A debt collector may not use any false, deceptive, or misleading representation or means in connection with the collection of any debt. Without limiting the general application of the foregoing, the following conduct is a violation of this section:

(1) The false representation or implication that the debt collector is vouched for, bonded by, or affiliated with the United States or any State, including the use of any badge, uniform, or facsimile thereof.

(2) The false representation of—

(A) the character, amount, or legal status of any debt; or

(B) any services rendered or compensation which may be lawfully received by any debt collector for the collection of a debt.

(3) The false representation or implication that any individual is an attorney or that any communication is from an attorney.

(4) The representation or implication that nonpayment of any debt will result in the arrest or imprisonment of any person or the seizure, garnishment, attachment, or sale of any property or wages of any person unless such action is lawful and the debt collector or creditor intends to take such action.

(5) The threat to take any action that cannot legally be taken or that is not intended to be taken.

(6) The false representation or implication that a sale, referral, or other transfer of any interest in a debt shall cause the consumer to—

(A) lose any claim or defense to payment of the debt; or

(B) become subject to any practice prohibited by this subchapter.

(7) The false representation or implication that the consumer committed any crime or other conduct in order to disgrace the consumer.

(8) Communicating or threatening to communicate to any person credit information which is known or which should be known to be false, including the failure to communicate that a disputed debt is disputed.

(9) The use or distribution of any written communication which simulates or is falsely represented to be a document authorized, issued, or approved by any court, official, or agency of the United States or any State, or which creates a false impression as to its source, authorization, or approval.

(10) The use of any false representation or deceptive means to collect or attempt to collect any debt or to obtain information concerning a consumer.

(11) The failure to disclose in the initial written communication with the consumer and, in addition, if the initial communication with the consumer is oral, in that initial oral communication, that the debt collector is attempting to collect a debt and that any information obtained will be used for that purpose, and the failure to disclose in subsequent communications that the communication is from a debt collector, except that this paragraph shall not apply to a formal pleading made in connection with a legal action.

(12) The false representation or implication that accounts have been turned over to innocent purchasers for value.

(13) The false representation or implication that documents are legal process.

(14) The use of any business, company, or organization name other than the true name of the debt collector's business, company, or organization.

(15) The false representation or implication that documents are not legal process forms or do not require action by the consumer.

(16) The false representation or implication that a debt collector operates or is employed by a consumer reporting agency as defined by section 1681a(f) of this title.

(Pub. L. 90–321, title VIII, §807, as added Pub. L. 95–109, Sept. 20, 1977, 91 Stat. 877; amended Pub. L. 104–208, div. A, title II, §2305(a), Sept. 30, 1996, 110 Stat. 3009–425.)

EDITORIAL NOTES

AMENDMENTS

1996—Par. (11). Pub. L. 104–208 amended par. (11) generally. Prior to amendment, par. (11) read as follows: "Except as otherwise provided for communications to acquire location information under section 1692b of this title, the failure to disclose clearly in all communications made to collect a debt or to obtain information about a consumer, that the debt collector is attempting to collect a debt and that any information obtained will be used for that purpose."

STATUTORY NOTES AND RELATED SUBSIDIARIES

EFFECTIVE DATE OF 1996 AMENDMENT

Pub. L. 104–208, div. A, title II, §2305(b), Sept. 30, 1996, 110 Stat. 3009–425, provided that: "The amendment made by subsection (a) [amending this section] shall take effect 90 days after the date of enactment of this Act [Sept. 30, 1996] and shall apply to all communications made after that date of enactment."

EFFECTIVE DATE

Section effective upon the expiration of six months after Sept. 20, 1977, see section 819 of Pub. L. 90–321, as added by Pub. L. 95–109, set out as a note under section 1692 of this title.

§1692f. Unfair practices

A debt collector may not use unfair or unconscionable means to collect or attempt to collect any debt. Without limiting the general application of the foregoing, the following conduct is a violation of this section:

(1) The collection of any amount (including any interest, fee, charge, or expense incidental to the principal obligation) unless such amount is expressly authorized by the agreement creating the debt or permitted by law.

(2) The acceptance by a debt collector from any person of a check or other payment instrument postdated by more than five days unless such person is notified in writing of the debt collector's intent to deposit such check or instrument not more than ten nor less than three business days prior to such deposit.

(3) The solicitation by a debt collector of any postdated check or other postdated payment instrument for the purpose of threatening or instituting criminal prosecution.

(4) Depositing or threatening to deposit any postdated check or other postdated payment instrument prior to the date on such check or instrument.

(5) Causing charges to be made to any person for communications by concealment of the true purpose of the communication. Such charges include, but are not limited to, collect telephone calls and telegram fees.

(6) Taking or threatening to take any nonjudicial action to effect dispossession or disablement of property if—

(A) there is no present right to possession of the property claimed as collateral through an enforceable security interest;

(B) there is no present intention to take possession of the property; or

(C) the property is exempt by law from such dispossession or disablement.

(7) Communicating with a consumer regarding a debt by post card.

(8) Using any language or symbol, other than the debt collector's address, on any envelope when communicating with a consumer by use of the mails or by telegram, except that a debt collector may use his business name if such name does not indicate that he is in the debt collection business.

(Pub. L. 90–321, title VIII, §808, as added Pub. L. 95–109, Sept. 20, 1977, 91 Stat. 879.)

STATUTORY NOTES AND RELATED SUBSIDIARIES

EFFECTIVE DATE

Section effective upon the expiration of six months after Sept. 20, 1977, see section 819 of Pub. L. 90–321, as added by Pub. L. 95–109, set out as a note under section 1692 of this title.

§1692g. Validation of debts

(a) Notice of debt; contents

Within five days after the initial communication with a consumer in connection with the collection of any debt, a debt collector shall, unless the following information is contained in the initial communication or the consumer has paid the debt, send the consumer a written notice containing—

(1) the amount of the debt;

(2) the name of the creditor to whom the debt is owed;

(3) a statement that unless the consumer, within thirty days after receipt of the notice, disputes the validity of the debt, or any portion thereof, the debt will be assumed to be valid by the debt collector;

(4) a statement that if the consumer notifies the debt collector in writing within the thirty-day period that the debt, or any portion thereof, is disputed, the debt collector will obtain verification of the debt or a copy of a judgment against the consumer and a copy of such verification or judgment will be mailed to the consumer by the debt collector; and

(5) a statement that, upon the consumer's written request within the thirty-day period, the debt collector will provide the consumer with the name and address of the original creditor, if different from the current creditor.

(b) Disputed debts

If the consumer notifies the debt collector in writing within the thirty-day period described in subsection (a) that the debt, or any portion thereof, is disputed, or that the consumer requests the name and address of the original creditor, the debt collector shall cease collection of the debt, or any disputed portion thereof, until the debt collector obtains verification of the debt or a copy of a judgment, or the name and address of the original creditor, and a copy of such verification or judgment, or name and address of the original creditor, is mailed to the consumer by the debt collector. Collection activities and communications that do not otherwise violate this subchapter may continue during the 30-day period referred to in subsection (a) unless the consumer has notified the debt collector in writing that the debt, or any portion of the debt, is disputed or that the consumer requests the name and address of the original creditor. Any collection activities and communication during the 30-day period may not overshadow or be inconsistent with the disclosure of the consumer's right to dispute the debt or request the name and address of the original creditor.

(c) Admission of liability

The failure of a consumer to dispute the validity of a debt under this section may not be construed by any court as an admission of liability by the consumer.

(d) Legal pleadings

A communication in the form of a formal pleading in a civil action shall not be treated as an initial communication for purposes of subsection (a).

(e) Notice provisions

The sending or delivery of any form or notice which does not relate to the collection of a debt and is expressly required by title 26, title V of Gramm-Leach-Bliley Act [15 U.S.C. 6801 et seq.], or any provision of Federal or State law relating to notice of data security breach or privacy, or any regulation prescribed under any such provision of law, shall not be treated as an initial communication in connection with debt collection for purposes of this section.

(Pub. L. 90–321, title VIII, §809, as added Pub. L. 95–109, Sept. 20, 1977, 91 Stat. 879; amended Pub. L. 109–351, title VIII, §802, Oct. 13, 2006, 120 Stat. 2006.)

REFERENCES IN TEXT

The Gramm-Leach-Bliley Act, referred to in subsec. (e), is Pub. L. 106–102, Nov. 12, 1999, 113 Stat. 1338. Title V of the Act is classified principally to chapter 94 (§ 6801 et seq.) of this title. For complete classification of this Act to the Code, see Short Title of 1999 Amendment note set out under section 1811 of Title 12, Banks and Banking, and Tables.

AMENDMENTS

2006—Subsec. (b). Pub. L. 109–351, §802(c), inserted at end "Collection activities and communications that do not otherwise violate this subchapter may continue during the 30-day period referred to in subsection (a) unless the consumer has notified the debt collector in writing that the debt, or any portion of the debt, is disputed or that the consumer requests the name and address of the original creditor. Any collection activities and communication during the 30-day period may not overshadow or be inconsistent with the disclosure of the consumer's right to dispute the debt or request the name and address of the original creditor."

Subsec. (d). Pub. L. 109–351, §802(a), added subsec. (d).

Subsec. (e). Pub. L. 109–351, §802(b), added subsec. (e).

STATUTORY NOTES AND RELATED SUBSIDIARIES

EFFECTIVE DATE

Section applicable only with respect to debts for which the initial attempt to collect occurs after the effective date of this subchapter, which takes effect upon the expiration of six months after Sept. 20, 1977, see section 819 of Pub. L. 90–321, as added by Pub. L. 95–109, set out as a note under section 1692 of this title.

§1692h. Multiple debts

If any consumer owes multiple debts and makes any single payment to any debt collector with respect to such debts, such debt collector may not apply such payment to any debt which is disputed by the consumer and, where applicable, shall apply such payment in accordance with the consumer's directions.

(Pub. L. 90–321, title VIII, §810, as added Pub. L. 95–109, Sept. 20, 1977, 91 Stat. 880.)

STATUTORY NOTES AND RELATED SUBSIDIARIES

EFFECTIVE DATE

Section effective upon the expiration of six months after Sept. 20, 1977, see section 819 of Pub. L. 90–321, as added by Pub. L. 95–109, set out as a note under section 1692 of this title.

§1692i. Legal actions by debt collectors

(a) Venue

Any debt collector who brings any legal action on a debt against any consumer shall—

(1) in the case of an action to enforce an interest in real property securing the consumer's obligation, bring such action only in a judicial district or similar legal entity in which such real property is located; or

(2) in the case of an action not described in paragraph (1), bring such action only in the judicial district or similar legal entity—

(A) in which such consumer signed the contract sued upon; or

(B) in which such consumer resides at the commencement of the action.

(b) Authorization of actions

Nothing in this subchapter shall be construed to authorize the bringing of legal actions by debt collectors.

(Pub. L. 90–321, title VIII, §811, as added Pub. L. 95–109, Sept. 20, 1977, 91 Stat. 880.)

EFFECTIVE DATE

Section effective upon the expiration of six months after Sept. 20, 1977, see section 819 of Pub. L. 90–321, as added by Pub. L. 95–109, set out as a note under section 1692 of this title.

§1692j. Furnishing certain deceptive forms

(a) It is unlawful to design, compile, and furnish any form knowing that such form would be used to create the false belief in a consumer that a person other than the creditor of such consumer is participating in the collection of or in an attempt to collect a debt such consumer allegedly owes such creditor, when in fact such person is not so participating.

(b) Any person who violates this section shall be liable to the same extent and in the same manner as a debt collector is liable under section 1692k of this title for failure to comply with a provision of this subchapter.

(Pub. L. 90–321, title VIII, §812, as added Pub. L. 95–109, Sept. 20, 1977, 91 Stat. 880.)

EFFECTIVE DATE

Section effective upon the expiration of six months after Sept. 20, 1977, see section 819 of Pub. L. 90–321, as added by Pub. L. 95–109, set out as a note under section 1692 of this title.

§1692k. Civil liability

(a) Amount of damages

Except as otherwise provided by this section, any debt collector who fails to comply with any provision of this subchapter with respect to any person is liable to such person in an amount equal to the sum of—

(1) any actual damage sustained by such person as a result of such failure;

(2)(A) in the case of any action by an individual, such additional damages as the court may allow, but not exceeding $1,000; or

(B) in the case of a class action, (i) such amount for each named plaintiff as could be recovered under subparagraph (A), and (ii) such amount as the court may allow for all other class members, without regard to a minimum individual recovery, not to exceed the lesser of $500,000 or 1 per centum of the net worth of the debt collector; and

(3) in the case of any successful action to enforce the foregoing liability, the costs of the action, together with a reasonable attorney's fee as determined by the court. On a finding by the court that an action under this section was brought in bad faith and for the purpose of harassment, the court may award to the defendant attorney's fees reasonable in relation to the work expended and costs.

(b) Factors considered by court

In determining the amount of liability in any action under subsection (a), the court shall consider, among other relevant factors—

(1) in any individual action under subsection (a)(2)(A), the frequency and persistence of noncompliance by the debt collector, the nature of such noncompliance, and the extent to which such noncompliance was intentional; or

(2) in any class action under subsection (a)(2)(B), the frequency and persistence of noncompliance by the debt collector, the nature of such noncompliance, the resources of the debt collector, the number of persons adversely affected, and the extent to which the debt collector's noncompliance was intentional.

(c) Intent

A debt collector may not be held liable in any action brought under this subchapter if the debt collector shows by a preponderance of evidence that the violation was not intentional and resulted from a bona fide error notwithstanding the maintenance of procedures reasonably adapted to avoid any such error.

(d) Jurisdiction

An action to enforce any liability created by this subchapter may be brought in any appropriate United States district court without regard to the amount in controversy, or in any other court of competent jurisdiction, within one year from the date on which the violation occurs.

(e) Advisory opinions of Bureau

No provision of this section imposing any liability shall apply to any act done or omitted in good faith in conformity with any advisory opinion of the Bureau, notwithstanding that after such act or omission has occurred, such opinion is amended, rescinded, or determined by judicial or other authority to be invalid for any reason.

(Pub. L. 90–321, title VIII, §813, as added Pub. L. 95–109, Sept. 20, 1977, 91 Stat. 881; amended Pub. L. 111–203, title X, §1089(1), July 21, 2010, 124 Stat. 2092.)

EDITORIAL NOTES

AMENDMENTS

2010—Subsec. (e). Pub. L. 111–203 substituted "Bureau" for "Commission".

STATUTORY NOTES AND RELATED SUBSIDIARIES

EFFECTIVE DATE OF 2010 AMENDMENT

Amendment by Pub. L. 111–203 effective on the designated transfer date, see section 1100H of Pub. L. 111–203, set out as a note under section 552a of Title 5, Government Organization and Employees.

EFFECTIVE DATE

Section effective upon the expiration of six months after Sept. 20, 1977, see section 819 of Pub. L. 90–321, as added by Pub. L. 95–109, set out as a note under section 1692 of this title.

§1692*l*. Administrative enforcement

(a) Federal Trade Commission

The Federal Trade Commission shall be authorized to enforce compliance with this subchapter, except to the extent that enforcement of the requirements imposed under this subchapter is specifically committed to another Government agency under any of paragraphs (1) through (5) of subsection (b), subject to subtitle B of the Consumer Financial Protection Act of 2010 [12 U.S.C. 5511 et seq.]. For purpose of the exercise by the Federal Trade Commission of its functions and powers under the Federal Trade Commission Act (15 U.S.C. 41 et seq.), a violation of this subchapter shall be deemed an unfair or deceptive act or practice in violation of that Act. All of the functions and powers of the Federal Trade Commission under the Federal Trade Commission Act are available to the Federal Trade Commission to enforce compliance by any person with this subchapter, irrespective of whether that person is engaged in commerce or meets any other jurisdictional tests under the Federal Trade Commission Act, including the power to enforce the provisions of this subchapter, in the same manner as if the violation had been a violation of a Federal Trade Commission trade regulation rule.

(b) Applicable provisions of law

Subject to subtitle B of the Consumer Financial Protection Act of 2010, compliance with any requirements imposed under this subchapter shall be enforced under—

(1) section 8 of the Federal Deposit Insurance Act [12 U.S.C. 1818], by the appropriate Federal banking agency, as defined in section 3(q) of the Federal Deposit Insurance Act (12 U.S.C. 1813(q)), with respect to—

(A) national banks, Federal savings associations, and Federal branches and Federal agencies of foreign banks;

(B) member banks of the Federal Reserve System (other than national banks), branches and agencies of foreign banks (other than Federal branches, Federal agencies, and insured State branches of foreign banks), commercial lending companies owned or controlled by foreign banks, and organizations operating under section 25 or 25A of the Federal Reserve Act [12 U.S.C. 601 et seq., 611 et seq.]; and

(C) banks and State savings associations insured by the Federal Deposit Insurance Corporation (other than members of the Federal Reserve System), and insured State branches of foreign banks;

(2) the Federal Credit Union Act [12 U.S.C. 1751 et seq.], by the Administrator of the National Credit Union Administration with respect to any Federal credit union;

(3) subtitle IV of title 49, by the Secretary of Transportation, with respect to all carriers subject to the jurisdiction of the Surface Transportation Board;

(4) part A of subtitle VII of title 49, by the Secretary of Transportation with respect to any air carrier or any foreign air carrier subject to that part;

(5) the Packers and Stockyards Act, 1921 [7 U.S.C. 181 et seq.] (except as provided in section 406 of that Act [7 U.S.C. 226, 227]), by the Secretary of Agriculture with respect to any activities subject to that Act; and

(6) subtitle E of the Consumer Financial Protection Act of 2010 [12 U.S.C. 5561 et seq.], by the Bureau, with respect to any person subject to this subchapter.

The terms used in paragraph (1) that are not defined in this subchapter or otherwise defined in section 3(s) of the Federal Deposit Insurance Act (12 U.S.C. 1813(s)) shall have the meaning given to them in section 1(b) of the International Banking Act of 1978 (12 U.S.C. 3101).

(c) Agency powers

For the purpose of the exercise by any agency referred to in subsection (b) of its powers under any Act referred to in that subsection, a violation of any requirement imposed under this subchapter shall be deemed to be a violation of a requirement imposed under that Act. In addition to its powers under any provision of law specifically referred to in subsection (b), each of the agencies referred to in that subsection may exercise, for the purpose of enforcing compliance with any requirement imposed under this subchapter any other authority conferred on it by law, except as provided in subsection (d).

(d) Rules and regulations

Except as provided in section 1029(a) of the Consumer Financial Protection Act of 2010 [12 U.S.C. 5519(a)], the Bureau may prescribe rules with respect to the collection of debts by debt collectors, as defined in this subchapter.

(Pub. L. 90–321, title VIII, §814, as added Pub. L. 95–109, Sept. 20, 1977, 91 Stat. 881; amended Pub. L. 98–443, §9(n), Oct. 4, 1984, 98 Stat. 1708; Pub. L. 101–73, title VII, §744(n), Aug. 9, 1989, 103 Stat. 440; Pub. L. 102–242, title II, §212(e), Dec. 19, 1991, 105 Stat. 2301; Pub. L. 102–550, title XVI, §1604(a)(8), Oct. 28, 1992, 106 Stat. 4082; Pub. L. 104–88, title III, §316, Dec. 29, 1995, 109 Stat. 949; Pub. L. 111–203, title X, §1089(3), (4), July 21, 2010, 124 Stat. 2092, 2093.)

EDITORIAL NOTES

REFERENCES IN TEXT

The Consumer Financial Protection Act of 2010, referred to in subsecs. (a) and (b), is title X of Pub. L. 111–203, July 21, 2010, 124 Stat. 1955. Subtitles B (§§1021–1029A) and E (§§1051–1058) of the Act are classified generally to parts B (§5511 et seq.) and E (§5561 et seq.), respectively, of subchapter V of chapter 53 of Title 12, Banks and Banking. For complete classification of subtitles B and E to the Code, see Tables.

The Federal Trade Commission Act, referred to in subsec. (a), is act Sept. 26, 1914, ch. 311, 38 Stat. 717, which is classified generally to subchapter I (§41 et seq.) of chapter 2 of this title. For complete classification of this Act to the Code, see section 58 of this title and Tables.

Sections 25 and 25A of the Federal Reserve Act, referred to in subsec. (b)(1)(B), are classified to subchapters I (§601 et seq.) and II (§611 et seq.), respectively, of chapter 6 of Title 12, Banks and Banking.

The Federal Credit Union Act, referred to in subsec. (b)(2), is act June 26, 1934, ch. 750, 48 Stat. 1216, which is classified generally to chapter 14 (§1751 et seq.) of Title 12. For complete classification of this Act to the Code, see section 1751 of Title 12 and Tables.

The Packers and Stockyards Act, 1921, referred to in subsec. (b)(5), is act Aug. 15, 1921, ch. 64, 42 Stat. 159, which is classified generally to chapter 9 (§181 et seq.) of Title 7, Agriculture. For complete classification of this Act to the Code, see section 181 of Title 7 and Tables.

CODIFICATION

In subsec. (b)(3), "subtitle IV of title 49" substituted for "the Acts to regulate commerce" on authority of Pub. L. 95–473, §3(b), Oct. 17, 1978, 92 Stat. 1466, the first section of which enacted subtitle IV of Title 49, Transportation.

In subsec. (b)(4), "part A of subtitle VII of title 49" substituted for "the Federal Aviation Act of 1958 [49 App. U.S.C. 1301 et seq.]" and "that part" substituted for "that Act" on authority of Pub. L. 103–272, §6(b), July 5, 1994, 108 Stat. 1378, the first section of which enacted subtitles II, III, and V to X of Title 49.

Section 1089(4) of Pub. L. 111–203, which directed amendment "in subsection (d)" of the Fair Debt Collection Practices Act, was executed in subsec. (d) of this section, which is section 814 of the Act, to reflect the probable intent of Congress. See 2010 Amendment note below.

AMENDMENTS

2010—Subsec. (a). Pub. L. 111–203, §1089(3)(A), added subsec. (a) and struck out former subsec. (a). Prior to amendment, text read as follows: "Compliance with this subchapter shall be enforced by the Commission, except to the extent that enforcement of the requirements imposed under this subchapter is specifically committed to another agency under subsection (b) of this section. For purpose of the exercise by the Commission of its functions and powers under the Federal Trade Commission Act, a violation of this subchapter shall be deemed an unfair or deceptive act or practice in violation of that Act. All of the functions and powers of the Commission under the Federal Trade Commission Act are available to the Commission to enforce compliance by any person with this subchapter, irrespective of whether that person is engaged in commerce or meets any other jurisdictional tests in the Federal Trade Commission Act, including the power to enforce the provisions of this subchapter in the same manner as if the violation had been a violation of a Federal Trade Commission trade regulation rule."

Subsec. (b). Pub. L. 111–203, §1089(3)(B)(i), substituted "Subject to subtitle B of the Consumer Financial Protection Act of 2010, compliance" for "Compliance" in introductory provisions.

Subsec. (b)(1). Pub. L. 111–203, §1089(3)(B)(ii), added par. (1) and struck out former par. (1) which read as follows: "section 8 of the Federal Deposit Insurance Act, in the case of—

"(A) national banks, and Federal branches and Federal agencies of foreign banks, by the Office of the Comptroller of the Currency;

"(B) member banks of the Federal Reserve System (other than national banks), branches and agencies of foreign banks (other than Federal branches, Federal agencies, and insured State branches of foreign banks), commercial lending companies owned or controlled by foreign banks, and organizations operating under section 25 or 25(a) of the Federal Reserve Act, by the Board of Governors of the Federal Reserve System; and

"(C) banks insured by the Federal Deposit Insurance Corporation (other than members of the Federal Reserve System) and insured State branches of foreign banks, by the Board of Directors of the Federal Deposit Insurance Corporation;".

Subsec. (b)(2) to (6). Pub. L. 111–203, §1089(3)(B)(ii)–(vi), added par. (6), redesignated former pars. (3) to (6) as (2) to (5), respectively, and struck out former par. (2) which read as follows: "section 8 of the Federal Deposit Insurance Act, by the Director of the Office of Thrift Supervision, in the case of a savings association the deposits of which are insured by the Federal Deposit Insurance Corporation;".

Subsec. (d). Pub. L. 111–203, §1089(4), substituted "Except as provided in section 1029(a) of the Consumer Financial Protection Act of 2010, the Bureau may prescribe rules with respect to the collection of debts by debt collectors, as defined in this subchapter" for "Neither the Commission nor any other agency referred to in subsection (b) of this section may promulgate trade regulation rules or other regulations with respect to the collection of debts by debt collectors as defined in this subchapter". See Codification note above.

1995—Subsec. (b)(4). Pub. L. 104–88 substituted "Secretary of Transportation, with respect to all carriers subject to the jurisdiction of the Surface Transportation Board" for "Interstate Commerce Commission with respect to any common carrier subject to those Acts".

1992—Subsec. (b)(1)(C). Pub. L. 102–550 substituted semicolon for period at end.

1991—Subsec. (b). Pub. L. 102–242, §212(e)(2), inserted at end "The terms used in paragraph (1) that are not defined in this subchapter or otherwise defined in section 3(s) of the Federal Deposit Insurance Act (12 U.S.C. 1813(s)) shall have the meaning given to them in section 1(b) of the International Banking Act of 1978 (12 U.S.C. 3101)."

Pub. L. 102–242, §212(e)(1), added par. (1) and struck out former par. (1) which read as follows: "section 8 of Federal Deposit Insurance Act, in the case of—

"(A) national banks, by the Comptroller of the Currency;

"(B) member banks of the Federal Reserve System (other than national banks), by the Federal Reserve Board; and

"(C) banks the deposits or accounts of which are insured by the Federal Deposit Insurance Corporation (other than members of the Federal Reserve System), by the Board of Directors of the Federal Deposit Insurance Corporation;".

1989—Subsec. (b)(2). Pub. L. 101–73 amended par. (2) generally. Prior to amendment, par. (2) read as follows: "section 5(d) of the Home Owners Loan Act of 1933, section 407 of the National Housing Act, and sections 6(i) and 17 of the Federal Home Loan Bank Act, by the Federal Home Loan Bank Board (acting directly or through the Federal Savings and Loan Insurance Corporation), in the case of any institution subject to any of those provisions;".

1984—Subsec. (b)(5). Pub. L. 98–443 substituted "Secretary of Transportation" for "Civil Aeronautics Board".

STATUTORY NOTES AND RELATED SUBSIDIARIES

EFFECTIVE DATE OF 2010 AMENDMENT

Amendment by Pub. L. 111–203 effective on the designated transfer date, see section 1100H of Pub. L. 111–203, set out as a note under section 552a of Title 5, Government Organization and Employees.

EFFECTIVE DATE OF 1995 AMENDMENT

Amendment by Pub. L. 104–88 effective Jan. 1, 1996, see section 2 of Pub. L. 104–88, set out as an Effective Date note under section 1301 of Title 49, Transportation.

EFFECTIVE DATE OF 1992 AMENDMENT

Amendment by Pub. L. 102–550 effective as if included in the Federal Deposit Insurance Corporation Improvement Act of 1991, Pub. L. 102–242, as of Dec. 19, 1991, see section 1609(a) of Pub. L. 102–550, set out as a note under section 191 of Title 12, Banks and Banking.

EFFECTIVE DATE OF 1984 AMENDMENT

Amendment by Pub. L. 98–443 effective Jan. 1, 1985, see section 9(v) of Pub. L. 98–443, set out as a note under section 5314 of Title 5, Government Organization and Employees.

EFFECTIVE DATE

Section effective upon the expiration of six months after Sept. 20, 1977, see section 819 of Pub. L. 90–321, as added by Pub. L. 95–109, set out as a note under section 1692 of this title.

TRANSFER OF FUNCTIONS

Functions vested in Administrator of National Credit Union Administration transferred and vested in National Credit Union Administration Board pursuant to section 1752a of Title 12, Banks and Banking.

§1692m. Reports to Congress by the Bureau; views of other Federal agencies

(a) Not later than one year after the effective date of this subchapter and at one-year intervals thereafter, the Bureau shall make reports to the Congress concerning the administration of its functions under this subchapter, including such recommendations as the Bureau deems necessary or appropriate. In addition, each report of the Bureau shall include its assessment of the extent to which compliance with this subchapter is being achieved and a summary of the enforcement actions taken by the Bureau under section 1692l of this title.

(b) In the exercise of its functions under this subchapter, the Bureau may obtain upon request the views of any other Federal agency which exercises enforcement functions under section 1692l of this title.

(Pub. L. 90–321, title VIII, §815, as added Pub. L. 95–109, Sept. 20, 1977, 91 Stat. 882; amended Pub. L. 111–203, title X, §1089(1), July 21, 2010, 124 Stat. 2092.)

EDITORIAL NOTES

REFERENCES IN TEXT

The effective date of this subchapter, referred to in subsec. (a), is the date occurring on expiration of six months after Sept. 20, 1977. See section 819 of Pub. L. 90–321, set out as an Effective Date note under section 1692 of this title.

AMENDMENTS

2010—Pub. L. 111–203 substituted "Bureau" for "Commission" wherever appearing.

STATUTORY NOTES AND RELATED SUBSIDIARIES

EFFECTIVE DATE OF 2010 AMENDMENT

Amendment by Pub. L. 111–203 effective on the designated transfer date, see section 1100H of Pub. L. 111–203, set out as a note under section 552a of Title 5, Government Organization and Employees.

EFFECTIVE DATE

Section effective upon the expiration of six months after Sept. 20, 1977, see section 819 of Pub. L. 90–321, as added by Pub. L. 95–109, set out as a note under section 1692 of this title.

§1692n. Relation to State laws

This subchapter does not annul, alter, or affect, or exempt any person subject to the provisions of this subchapter from complying with the laws of any State with respect to debt collection practices, except to the extent that those laws are inconsistent with any provision of this subchapter, and then only to the extent of the inconsistency. For purposes of this section, a State law is not inconsistent with this subchapter if the protection such law affords any consumer is greater than the protection provided by this subchapter.

(Pub. L. 90–321, title VIII, §816, as added Pub. L. 95–109, Sept. 20, 1977, 91 Stat. 883.)

EFFECTIVE DATE

Section effective upon the expiration of six months after Sept. 20, 1977, see section 819 of Pub. L. 90–321, as added by Pub. L. 95–109, set out as a note under section 1692 of this title.

§1692o. Exemption for State regulation

The Bureau shall by regulation exempt from the requirements of this subchapter any class of debt collection practices within any State if the Bureau determines that under the law of that State that class of debt collection practices is subject to requirements substantially similar to those imposed by this subchapter, and that there is adequate provision for enforcement.

(Pub. L. 90–321, title VIII, §817, as added Pub. L. 95–109, Sept. 20, 1977, 91 Stat. 883; amended Pub. L. 111–203, title X, §1089(1), July 21, 2010, 124 Stat. 2092.)

EDITORIAL NOTES

AMENDMENTS

2010—Pub. L. 111–203 substituted "Bureau" for "Commission" in two places.

EFFECTIVE DATE OF 2010 AMENDMENT

Amendment by Pub. L. 111–203 effective on the designated transfer date, see section 1100H of Pub. L. 111–203, set out as a note under section 552a of Title 5, Government Organization and Employees.

EFFECTIVE DATE

Section effective upon the expiration of six months after Sept. 20, 1977, see section 819 of Pub. L. 90–321, as added by Pub. L. 95–109, set out as a note under section 1692 of this title.

§1692p. Exception for certain bad check enforcement programs operated by private entities

(a) In general

(1) Treatment of certain private entities

Subject to paragraph (2), a private entity shall be excluded from the definition of a debt collector, pursuant to the exception provided in section 1692a(6) of this title, with respect to the operation by the entity of a program described in paragraph (2)(A) under a contract described in paragraph (2)(B).

(2) Conditions of applicability

Paragraph (1) shall apply if—

(A) a State or district attorney establishes, within the jurisdiction of such State or district attorney and with respect to alleged bad check violations that do not involve a check described in subsection (b), a pretrial diversion program for alleged bad check offenders who agree to participate voluntarily in such program to avoid criminal prosecution;

(B) a private entity, that is subject to an administrative support services contract with a State or district attorney and operates under the direction, supervision, and control of such State or district attorney, operates the pretrial diversion program described in subparagraph (A); and

(C) in the course of performing duties delegated to it by a State or district attorney under the contract, the private entity referred to in subparagraph (B)—

(i) complies with the penal laws of the State;

(ii) conforms with the terms of the contract and directives of the State or district attorney;

(iii) does not exercise independent prosecutorial discretion;

(iv) contacts any alleged offender referred to in subparagraph (A) for purposes of participating in a program referred to in such paragraph—

(I) only as a result of any determination by the State or district attorney that probable cause of a bad check violation under State penal law exists, and that contact with the alleged offender for purposes of participation in the program is appropriate; and

(II) the alleged offender has failed to pay the bad check after demand for payment, pursuant to State law, is made for payment of the check amount;

(v) includes as part of an initial written communication with an alleged offender a clear and conspicuous statement that—

(I) the alleged offender may dispute the validity of any alleged bad check violation;

(II) where the alleged offender knows, or has reasonable cause to believe, that the alleged bad check violation is the result of theft or forgery of the check, identity theft, or other fraud that is not the result of the conduct of the alleged offender, the alleged offender may file a crime report with the appropriate law enforcement agency; and

(III) if the alleged offender notifies the private entity or the district attorney in writing, not later than 30 days after being contacted for the first time pursuant to clause (iv), that there is a dispute pursuant to this subsection, before further restitution efforts are pursued, the district attorney or an employee of the district attorney authorized to make such a determination makes a determination that there is probable cause to believe that a crime has been committed; and

(vi) charges only fees in connection with services under the contract that have been authorized by the contract with the State or district attorney.

(b) Certain checks excluded

A check is described in this subsection if the check involves, or is subsequently found to involve—

(1) a postdated check presented in connection with a payday loan, or other similar transaction, where the payee of the check knew that the issuer had insufficient funds at the time the check was made, drawn, or delivered;

(2) a stop payment order where the issuer acted in good faith and with reasonable cause in stopping payment on the check;

(3) a check dishonored because of an adjustment to the issuer's account by the financial institution holding such account without providing notice to the person at the time the check was made, drawn, or delivered;

(4) a check for partial payment of a debt where the payee had previously accepted partial payment for such debt;

(5) a check issued by a person who was not competent, or was not of legal age, to enter into a legal contractual obligation at the time the check was made, drawn, or delivered; or

(6) a check issued to pay an obligation arising from a transaction that was illegal in the jurisdiction of the State or district attorney at the time the check was made, drawn, or delivered.

(c) Definitions

For purposes of this section, the following definitions shall apply:

(1) State or district attorney

The term "State or district attorney" means the chief elected or appointed prosecuting attorney in a district, county (as defined in section 2 of title 1), municipality, or comparable jurisdiction, including State attorneys general who act as chief elected or appointed prosecuting attorneys in a district, county (as so defined), municipality or comparable jurisdiction, who may be referred to by a variety of titles such as district attorneys, prosecuting attorneys, commonwealth's attorneys, solicitors, county attorneys, and state's attorneys, and who are responsible for the prosecution of State crimes and violations of jurisdiction-specific local ordinances.

(2) Check

The term "check" has the same meaning as in section 5002(6) of title 12.

(3) Bad check violation

The term "bad check violation" means a violation of the applicable State criminal law relating to the writing of dishonored checks.

(Pub. L. 90–321, title VIII, §818, as added Pub. L. 109–351, title VIII, §801(a)(2), Oct. 13, 2006, 120 Stat. 2004.)

This marks the end of the Fair Debt Collection Practices Act
U.S.C. 15 §§ 1692-1692p

ELECTRONIC FUND TRANSFER ACT

15 U.S.C. §§ 1693-1693r, as amended

This Act (Title IX of the Consumer Credit Protection Act) establishes the rights, liabilities and responsibilities of participants in electronic fund transfer systems. The Act requires financial institutions to adopt certain practices respecting such matters as transaction accounting, and error resolution, requires financial institutions and others to have certain procedures for preauthorized transfers, and sets liability limits for losses caused by unauthorized transfers. The Credit CARD Act and the Dodd-Frank Act made substantial amendments to this Act.

Revised
January 2024

SUBCHAPTER VI—ELECTRONIC FUND TRANSFERS

§1693. Congressional findings and declaration of purpose

(a) Rights and liabilities undefined

The Congress finds that the use of electronic systems to transfer funds provides the potential for substantial benefits to consumers. However, due to the unique characteristics of such systems, the application of existing consumer protection legislation is unclear, leaving the rights and liabilities of consumers, financial institutions, and intermediaries in electronic fund transfers undefined.

(b) Purposes

It is the purpose of this subchapter to provide a basic framework establishing the rights, liabilities, and responsibilities of participants in electronic fund and remittance transfer systems. The primary objective of this subchapter, however, is the provision of individual consumer rights.

(Pub. L. 90–321, title IX, §902, as added Pub. L. 95–630, title XX, §2001, Nov. 10, 1978, 92 Stat. 3728; amended Pub. L. 111–203, title X, §1073(a)(1), July 21, 2010, 124 Stat. 2060.)

EDITORIAL NOTES

AMENDMENTS

2010—Subsec. (b). Pub. L. 111–203 inserted "and remittance" after "electronic fund".

STATUTORY NOTES AND RELATED SUBSIDIARIES

EFFECTIVE DATE OF 2010 AMENDMENT

Amendment by Pub. L. 111–203 effective 1 day after July 21, 2010, except as otherwise provided, see section 4 of Pub. L. 111–203, set out as an Effective Date note under section 5301 of Title 12, Banks and Banking.

EFFECTIVE DATE

Pub. L. 90–321, title IX, §923, formerly §921, as added by Pub. L. 95–630, title XX, §2001, Nov. 10, 1978, 92 Stat. 3741, renumbered §922, Pub. L. 111–24, title IV, §401(1), May 22, 2009, 123 Stat. 1751; renumbered §923, Pub. L. 111–203, title X, §1073(a)(3), July 21, 2010, 124 Stat. 2060, provided that: "This title [enacting this subchapter] takes effect upon the expiration of eighteen months from the date of its enactment [Nov. 10, 1978], except that sections 909 and 911 [sections 1693g, 1693i of this title] take effect upon the expiration of ninety days after the date of enactment."

[Pub. L. 111–203, §1073(a)(3), which directed renumbering of section 922 of Pub. L. 90–321 as section 923 effective 1 day after July 21, 2010, was executed after the renumbering of section 921 of Pub. L. 90–321 as section 922 by Pub. L. 111–24, §401(1), effective 15 months after May 22, 2009, to reflect the probable intent of Congress.]

SHORT TITLE

This subchapter known as the "Electronic Fund Transfer Act", see Short Title note set out under section 1601 of this title.

§1693a. Definitions

As used in this subchapter—

(1) the term "accepted card or other means of access" means a card, code, or other means of access to a consumer's account for the purpose of initiating electronic fund transfers when the person to whom such card or other means of access was issued has requested and received or has signed or has used, or authorized another to use, such card or other means of access for the purpose of transferring money between accounts or obtaining money, property, labor, or services;

(2) the term "account" means a demand deposit, savings deposit, or other asset account (other than an occasional or incidental credit balance in an open end credit plan as defined in section 1602(i) [1] of this title), as described in regulations of the Bureau, established primarily for personal, family, or household purposes, but such term does not include an account held by a financial institution pursuant to a bona fide trust agreement;

(4) [2] the term "Board" means the Board of Governors of the Federal Reserve System;

(4) [2] the term "Bureau" means the Bureau of Consumer Financial Protection;

(5) the term "business day" means any day on which the offices of the consumer's financial institution involved in an electronic fund transfer are open to the public for carrying on substantially all of its business functions;

(6) the term "consumer" means a natural person;

(7) the term "electronic fund transfer" means any transfer of funds, other than a transaction originated by check, draft, or similar paper instrument, which is initiated through an electronic terminal, telephonic instrument, or computer or magnetic tape so as to order, instruct, or authorize a financial institution to debit or credit an account. Such term includes, but is not limited to, point-of-sale transfers, automated teller machine transactions, direct deposits or withdrawals of funds, and transfers initiated by telephone. Such term does not include—

(A) any check guarantee or authorization service which does not directly result in a debit or credit to a consumer's account: [3]

(B) any transfer of funds, other than those processed by automated clearinghouse, made by a financial institution on behalf of a consumer by means of a service that transfers funds held at either Federal Reserve banks or other depository institutions and which is not designed primarily to transfer funds on behalf of a consumer;

(C) any transaction the primary purpose of which is the purchase or sale of securities or commodities through a broker-dealer registered with or regulated by the Securities and Exchange Commission;

(D) any automatic transfer from a savings account to a demand deposit account pursuant to an agreement between a consumer and a financial institution for the purpose of covering an overdraft or maintaining an agreed upon minimum balance in the consumer's demand deposit account; or

(E) any transfer of funds which is initiated by a telephone conversation between a consumer and an officer or employee of a financial institution which is not pursuant to a prearranged plan and under which periodic or recurring transfers are not contemplated;

as determined under regulations of the Bureau;

(8) the term "electronic terminal" means an electronic device, other than a telephone operated by a consumer, through which a consumer may initiate an electronic fund transfer. Such term includes, but is not limited to, point-of-sale terminals, automated teller machines, and cash dispensing machines;

(9) the term "financial institution" means a State or National bank, a State or Federal savings and loan association, a mutual savings bank, a State or Federal credit union, or any other person who, directly or indirectly, holds an account belonging to a consumer;

(10) the term "preauthorized electronic fund transfer" means an electronic fund transfer authorized in advance to recur at substantially regular intervals;

(11) the term "State" means any State, territory, or possession of the United States, the District of Columbia, the Commonwealth of Puerto Rico, or any political subdivision of any of the foregoing; and

(12) the term "unauthorized electronic fund transfer" means an electronic fund transfer from a consumer's account initiated by a person other than the consumer without actual authority to initiate such transfer and from which the consumer receives no benefit, but the term does not include any electronic fund transfer (A) initiated by a person other than the consumer who was furnished with the card, code, or other means of access to such consumer's account by such consumer, unless the consumer has notified the financial institution involved that transfers by such other person are no longer authorized, (B) initiated with fraudulent intent by the consumer or any person acting in concert with the consumer, or (C) which constitutes an error committed by a financial institution.

(Pub. L. 90–321, title IX, §903, as added Pub. L. 95–630, title XX, §2001, Nov. 10, 1978, 92 Stat. 3728; amended Pub. L. 111–203, title X, §1084(1), (2), July 21, 2010, 124 Stat. 2081.)

EDITORIAL NOTES

REFERENCES IN TEXT

Section 1602(i) of this title, referred to in par. (2), was redesignated section 1602(j) of this title by Pub. L. 111–203, title X, §1100A(1)(A), July 21, 2010, 124 Stat. 2107.

AMENDMENTS

2010—Pub. L. 111–203, §1084(1), which directed the substitution of "Bureau" for "Board" wherever appearing, was executed by making the substitution in pars. (2) and (6) but not in par. (3), to reflect the probable intent of Congress.

Par. (3). Pub. L. 111–203, §1084(2)(A), redesignated par. (3) as (4) defining the term "Board".

Par. (4). Pub. L. 111–203, §1084(2)(B), which directed addition of par. (4) defining the term "Bureau" after par. (3), was executed by making the addition after par. (4) defining the term "Board", to reflect the probable intent of Congress.

Pub. L. 111–203, §1084(2)(A), redesignated par. (3) as (4) defining the term "Board". Former par. (4) redesignated (5).

Pars. (5) to (12). Pub. L. 111–203, §1084(2)(A), redesignated pars. (4) to (11) as (5) to (12), respectively.

STATUTORY NOTES AND RELATED SUBSIDIARIES

EFFECTIVE DATE OF 2010 AMENDMENT

Amendment by Pub. L. 111–203 effective on the designated transfer date, see section 1100H of Pub. L. 111–203, set out as a note under section 552a of Title 5, Government Organization and Employees.

[1] See References in Text note below.

[2] So in original. There are two pars. designated "(4)" and no par. (3).

[3] So in original. The colon probably should be a semicolon.

§1693b. Regulations

(a) Prescription by the Bureau and the Board

(1) In general

Except as provided in paragraph (2), the Bureau shall prescribe rules to carry out the purposes of this subchapter.

(2) Authority of the Board

The Board shall have sole authority to prescribe rules—

(A) to carry out the purposes of this subchapter with respect to a person described in section 5519(a) of title 12; and

(B) to carry out the purposes of section 1693o–2 of this title.

In prescribing such regulations, the Board shall:

(1) [1] consult with the other agencies referred to in section 1693o [2] of this title and take into account, and allow for, the continuing evolution of electronic banking services and the technology utilized in such services,

(2) [1] prepare an analysis of economic impact which considers the costs and benefits to financial institutions, consumers, and other users of electronic fund transfers, including the extent to which additional documentation, reports, records, or other paper work would be required, and the effects upon competition in the provision of electronic banking services among large and small financial institutions and the availability of such services to different classes of consumers, particularly low income consumers,

(3) [1] to the extent practicable, the Board shall demonstrate that the consumer protections of the proposed regulations outweigh the compliance costs imposed upon consumers and financial institutions, and

(4) [1] any proposed regulations and accompanying analyses shall be sent promptly to Congress by the Board.

(b) Issuance of model clauses

The Bureau shall issue model clauses for optional use by financial institutions to facilitate compliance with the disclosure requirements of section 1693c of this title and to aid consumers in understanding the rights and responsibilities of participants in electronic fund transfers by utilizing readily understandable language. Such model clauses shall be adopted after notice duly given in the Federal Register and opportunity for public comment in accordance with section 553 of title 5. With respect to the disclosures required by section 1693c(a)(3) and (4) of this title, the Bureau shall take account of variations in the services and charges under different electronic fund transfer systems and, as appropriate, shall issue alternative model clauses for disclosure of these differing account terms.

(c) Criteria; modification of requirements

Regulations prescribed hereunder may contain such classifications, differentiations, or other provisions, and may provide for such adjustments and exceptions for any class of electronic fund transfers or remittance transfers, as in the judgment of the Bureau are necessary or proper to effectuate the purposes of this subchapter, to prevent circumvention or evasion thereof, or to facilitate compliance therewith. The Bureau shall by regulation modify the requirements imposed by this subchapter on small financial institutions if the Bureau determines that such modifications are necessary to alleviate any undue compliance burden on small financial institutions and such modifications are consistent with the purpose and objective of this subchapter.

(d) Applicability to service providers other than certain financial institutions

(1) In general

If electronic fund transfer services are made available to consumers by a person other than a financial institution holding a consumer's account, the Bureau shall by regulation assure that the disclosures, protections, responsibilities, and remedies created by this subchapter are made applicable to such persons and services.

(2) State and local government electronic benefit transfer systems

(A) "Electronic benefit transfer system" defined

In this paragraph, the term "electronic benefit transfer system"—

(i) means a system under which a government agency distributes needs-tested benefits by establishing accounts that may be accessed by recipients electronically, such as through automated teller machines or point-of-sale terminals; and

(ii) does not include employment-related payments, including salaries and pension, retirement, or unemployment benefits established by a Federal, State, or local government agency.

(B) Exemption generally

The disclosures, protections, responsibilities, and remedies established under this subchapter, and any regulation prescribed or order issued by the Bureau in accordance with this subchapter, shall not apply to any electronic benefit transfer system established under State or local law or administered by a State or local government.

(C) Exception for direct deposit into recipient's account

Subparagraph (B) shall not apply with respect to any electronic funds transfer under an electronic benefit transfer system for a deposit directly into a consumer account held by the recipient of the benefit.

(D) Rule of construction

No provision of this paragraph—

(i) affects or alters the protections otherwise applicable with respect to benefits established by any other provision [3] Federal, State, or local law; or

(ii) otherwise supersedes the application of any State or local law.

(3) Fee disclosures at automated teller machines

(A) In general

The regulations prescribed under paragraph (1) shall require any automated teller machine operator who imposes a fee on any consumer for providing host transfer services to such consumer to provide notice in accordance with subparagraph (B) to the consumer (at the time the service is provided) of—

(i) the fact that a fee is imposed by such operator for providing the service; and

(ii) the amount of any such fee.

(B) Notice requirement

The notice required under clauses (i) and (ii) of subparagraph (A) with respect to any fee described in such subparagraph shall appear on the screen of the automated teller machine, or on a paper notice issued from such machine, after the transaction is initiated and before the consumer is irrevocably committed to completing the transaction.

(C) Prohibition on fees not properly disclosed and explicitly assumed by consumer

No fee may be imposed by any automated teller machine operator in connection with any electronic fund transfer initiated by a consumer for which a notice is required under subparagraph (A), unless—

(i) the consumer receives such notice in accordance with subparagraph (B); and

(ii) the consumer elects to continue in the manner necessary to effect the transaction after receiving such notice.

(D) Definitions

For purposes of this paragraph, the following definitions shall apply:

(i) Automated teller machine operator

The term "automated teller machine operator" means any person who—

(I) operates an automated teller machine at which consumers initiate electronic fund transfers; and

(II) is not the financial institution that holds the account of such consumer from which the transfer is made.

(ii) Electronic fund transfer

The term "electronic fund transfer" includes a transaction that involves a balance inquiry initiated by a consumer in the same manner as an electronic fund transfer, whether or not the consumer initiates a transfer of funds in the course of the transaction.

(iii) Host transfer services

The term "host transfer services" means any electronic fund transfer made by an automated teller machine operator in connection with a transaction initiated by a consumer at an automated teller machine operated by such operator.

(e) Deference

No provision of this subchapter may be construed as altering, limiting, or otherwise affecting the deference that a court affords to—

(1) the Bureau in making determinations regarding the meaning or interpretation of any provision of this subchapter for which the Bureau has authority to prescribe regulations; or

(2) the Board in making determinations regarding the meaning or interpretation of section 1693o–2 of this title.

(Pub. L. 90–321, title IX, §904, as added Pub. L. 95–630, title XX, §2001, Nov. 10, 1978, 92 Stat. 3730; amended Pub. L. 104–193, title VIII, §891, title IX, §907, Aug. 22, 1996, 110 Stat. 2346, 2350; Pub. L. 106–102, title VII, §702, Nov. 12, 1999, 113 Stat. 1463; Pub. L. 111–203, title X, §§1073(a)(2), 1084(1), (3), July 21, 2010, 124 Stat. 2060, 2081; Pub. L. 112–216, §1, Dec. 20, 2012, 126 Stat. 1590.)

EDITORIAL NOTES

REFERENCES IN TEXT

Section 1693o of this title, referred to in subsec. (a)(1), was in the original "section 917", and was translated as meaning section 918 of Pub. L. 90–321 to reflect the probable intent of Congress and the renumbering of section 917 of Pub. L. 90–321 as section 918 by Pub. L. 111–24, title IV, §401, May 22, 2009, 123 Stat. 1751.

AMENDMENTS

2012—Subsec. (d)(3)(B). Pub. L. 112–216, in subpar. heading, substituted "requirement" for "requirements" and, in text, substituted "The notice required under clauses (i) and (ii)" for

"(i) ON THE MACHINE.—The notice required under clause (i) of subparagraph (A) with respect to any fee described in such subparagraph shall be posted in a prominent and conspicuous location on or at the automated teller machine at which the electronic fund transfer is initiated by the consumer.

"(ii) ON THE SCREEN.—The notice required under clauses (i) and (ii)" and struck out ", except that during the period beginning on November 12, 1999, and ending on December 31, 2004, this clause shall not apply to any automated teller machine that lacks the technical capability to disclose the notice on the screen or to issue a paper notice after the transaction is initiated and before the consumer is irrevocably committed to completing the transaction" after "completing the transaction".

2010—Pub. L. 111–203, §1084(1), substituted "Bureau" for "Board" wherever appearing in subsecs. (b) to (d).

Subsec. (a). Pub. L. 111–203, §1084(3)(A), substituted "Prescription by the Bureau and the Board" for "Prescription by Board" in heading that had been supplied editorially and substituted initial pars. (1) and (2), relating to the Bureau's prescription of rules and authority of the Board, for first sentence of former introductory provisions which read as follows: "The Board shall prescribe regulations to carry out the purposes of this subchapter." Second sentence of former introductory provisions was redesignated as concluding provisions of par. (2) to reflect the probable intent of Congress.

Subsec. (c). Pub. L. 111–203, §1073(a)(2), inserted "or remittance transfers" after "electronic fund transfers".

Subsec. (e). Pub. L. 111–203, §1084(3)(B), added subsec. (e).

1999—Subsec. (d)(3). Pub. L. 106–102 added par. (3).

1996—Subsec. (d). Pub. L. 104–193, §907, which directed the amendment of subsec. (d), was not executed because of similar amendment by Pub. L. 104–193, §891. See below. Section 907 of Pub. L. 104–193 provided that subsec. (d) was to be amended by inserting subsec. (d) heading, by designating existing provisions as par. (1) and inserting heading, and by adding a new par. (2) reading as follows:

"(2) STATE AND LOCAL GOVERNMENT ELECTRONIC BENEFIT TRANSFER PROGRAMS.—

"(A) EXEMPTION GENERALLY.—The disclosures, protections, responsibilities, and remedies established under this subchapter, and any regulation prescribed or order issued by the Board in accordance with this subchapter, shall not apply to any electronic benefit transfer program established under State or local law or administered by a State or local government.

"(B) Exception for direct deposit into recipient's account.—Subparagraph (A) shall not apply with respect to any electronic funds transfer under an electronic benefit transfer program for deposits directly into a consumer account held by the recipient of the benefit.

"(C) Rule of construction.—No provision of this paragraph may be construed as—

"(i) affecting or altering the protections otherwise applicable with respect to benefits established by Federal, State, or local law; or

"(ii) otherwise superseding the application of any State or local law.

"(D) Electronic benefit transfer program defined.—For purposes of this paragraph, the term 'electronic benefit transfer program'—

"(i) means a program under which a government agency distributes needs-tested benefits by establishing accounts to be accessed by recipients electronically, such as through automated teller machines, or point-of-sale terminals; and

"(ii) does not include employment-related payments, including salaries and pension, retirement, or unemployment benefits established by Federal, State, or local governments."

Pub. L. 104–193, §891, designated existing provisions as par. (1), inserted subsec. heading and par. (2), and substituted "If" for "In the event that".

STATUTORY NOTES AND RELATED SUBSIDIARIES

EFFECTIVE DATE OF 2010 AMENDMENT

Amendment by section 1073(a)(2) of Pub. L. 111–203 effective 1 day after July 21, 2010, except as otherwise provided, see section 4 of Pub. L. 111–203, set out as an Effective Date note under section 5301 of Title 12, Banks and Banking.

Amendment by section 1084(1), (3) of Pub. L. 111–203 effective on the designated transfer date, see section 1100H of Pub. L. 111–203, set out as a note under section 552a of Title 5, Government Organization and Employees.

[1] So in original. See 2010 Amendment note below.

[2] See References in Text note below.

[3] So in original. Probably should be followed by "of".

§1693c. Terms and conditions of transfers

(a) Disclosures; time; form; contents

The terms and conditions of electronic fund transfers involving a consumer's account shall be disclosed at the time the consumer contracts for an electronic fund transfer service, in accordance with regulations of the Bureau. Such disclosures shall be in readily understandable language and shall include, to the extent applicable—

(1) the consumer's liability for unauthorized electronic fund transfers and, at the financial institution's option, notice of the advisability of prompt reporting of any loss, theft, or unauthorized use of a card, code, or other means of access;

(2) the telephone number and address of the person or office to be notified in the event the consumer believes than [1] an unauthorized electronic fund transfer has been or may be effected;

(3) the type and nature of electronic fund transfers which the consumer may initiate, including any limitations on the frequency or dollar amount of such transfers, except that the details of such limitations need not be disclosed if their confidentiality is necessary to maintain the security of an electronic fund transfer system, as determined by the Bureau;

(4) any charges for electronic fund transfers or for the right to make such transfers;

(5) the consumer's right to stop payment of a preauthorized electronic fund transfer and the procedure to initiate such a stop payment order;

(6) the consumer's right to receive documentation of electronic fund transfers under section 1693d of this title;

(7) a summary, in a form prescribed by regulations of the Bureau, of the error resolution provisions of section 1693f of this title and the consumer's rights thereunder. The financial institution shall thereafter transmit such summary at least once per calendar year;

(8) the financial institution's liability to the consumer under section 1693h of this title;

(9) under what circumstances the financial institution will in the ordinary course of business disclose information concerning the consumer's account to third persons; and

(10) a notice to the consumer that a fee may be imposed by—

    (A) an automated teller machine operator (as defined in section 1693b(d)(3)(D)(i) of this title) if the consumer initiates a transfer from an automated teller machine that is not operated by the person issuing the card or other means of access; and

    (B) any national, regional, or local network utilized to effect the transaction.

(b) Notification of changes to consumer

A financial institution shall notify a consumer in writing at least twenty-one days prior to the effective date of any change in any term or condition of the consumer's account required to be disclosed under subsection (a) if such change would result in greater cost or liability for such consumer or decreased access to the consumer's account. A financial institution may, however, implement a change in the terms or conditions of an account without prior notice when such change is immediately necessary to maintain or restore the security of an electronic fund transfer system or a consumer's account. Subject to subsection (a)(3), the Bureau shall require subsequent notification if such a change is made permanent.

(c) Time for disclosures respecting accounts accessible prior to effective date of this subchapter

For any account of a consumer made accessible to electronic fund transfers prior to the effective date of this subchapter, the information required to be disclosed to the consumer under subsection (a) shall be disclosed not later than the earlier of—

    (1) the first periodic statement required by section 1693d(c) of this title after the effective date of this subchapter; or

    (2) thirty days after the effective date of this subchapter.

(Pub. L. 90–321, title IX, §905, as added Pub. L. 95–630, title XX, §2001, Nov. 10, 1978, 92 Stat. 3730; amended Pub. L. 106–102, title VII, §703, Nov. 12, 1999, 113 Stat. 1464; Pub. L. 111–203, title X, §1084(1), July 21, 2010, 124 Stat. 2081.)

EDITORIAL NOTES

REFERENCES IN TEXT

For effective date of this subchapter, referred to in subsec. (c), see section 921 of Pub. L. 90–321, set out as an Effective Date note under section 1693 of this title.

AMENDMENTS

2010—Subsecs. (a), (b). Pub. L. 111–203 substituted "Bureau" for "Board" wherever appearing.
1999—Subsec. (a)(10). Pub. L. 106–102 added par. (10).

STATUTORY NOTES AND RELATED SUBSIDIARIES

EFFECTIVE DATE OF 2010 AMENDMENT

Amendment by Pub. L. 111–203 effective on the designated transfer date, see section 1100H of Pub. L. 111–203, set out as a note under section 552a of Title 5, Government Organization and Employees.

  [1] So in original. Probably should be "that".

§1693d. Documentation of transfers

(a) Availability of written documentation to consumer; contents

For each electronic fund transfer initiated by a consumer from an electronic terminal, the financial institution holding such consumer's account shall, directly or indirectly, at the time the transfer is initiated, make available to the consumer written documentation of such transfer. The documentation shall clearly set forth to the extent applicable—

    (1) the amount involved and date the transfer is initiated;

    (2) the type of transfer;

    (3) the identity of the consumer's account with the financial institution from which or to which funds are transferred;

    (4) the identity of any third party to whom or from whom funds are transferred; and

    (5) the location or identification of the electronic terminal involved.

(b) Notice of credit to consumer

For a consumer's account which is scheduled to be credited by a preauthorized electronic fund transfer from the same payor at least once in each successive sixty-day period, except where the payor provides positive notice of the transfer to the consumer, the financial institution shall elect to provide promptly either positive notice to the consumer when the credit is made as scheduled, or negative notice to the consumer when the credit is not made as scheduled, in accordance with regulations of the Bureau. The means of notice elected shall be disclosed to the consumer in accordance with section 1693c of this title.

(c) Periodic statement; contents

A financial institution shall provide each consumer with a periodic statement for each account of such consumer that may be accessed by means of an electronic fund transfer. Except as provided in subsections (d) and (e), such statement shall be provided at least monthly for each monthly or shorter cycle in which an electronic fund transfer affecting the account has occurred, or every three months, whichever is more frequent. The statement, which may include information regarding transactions other than electronic fund transfers, shall clearly set forth—

(1) with regard to each electronic fund transfer during the period, the information described in subsection (a), which may be provided on an accompanying document;

(2) the amount of any fee or charge assessed by the financial institution during the period for electronic fund transfers or for account maintenance;

(3) the balances in the consumer's account at the beginning of the period and at the close of the period; and

(4) the address and telephone number to be used by the financial institution for the purpose of receiving any statement inquiry or notice of account error from the consumer. Such address and telephone number shall be preceded by the caption "Direct Inquiries To:" or other similar language indicating that the address and number are to be used for such inquiries or notices.

(d) Consumer passbook accounts

In the case of a consumer's passbook account which may not be accessed by electronic fund transfers other than preauthorized electronic fund transfers crediting the account, a financial institution may, in lieu of complying with the requirements of subsection (c), upon presentation of the passbook provide the consumer in writing with the amount and date of each such transfer involving the account since the passbook was last presented.

(e) Accounts other than passbook accounts

In the case of a consumer's account, other than a passbook account, which may not be accessed by electronic fund transfers other than preauthorized electronic fund transfers crediting the account, the financial institution may provide a periodic statement on a quarterly basis which otherwise complies with the requirements of subsection (c).

(f) Documentation as evidence

In any action involving a consumer, any documentation required by this section to be given to the consumer which indicates that an electronic fund transfer was made to another person shall be admissible as evidence of such transfer and shall constitute prima facie proof that such transfer was made.

(Pub. L. 90–321, title IX, §906, as added Pub. L. 95–630, title XX, §2001, Nov. 10, 1978, 92 Stat. 3731; amended Pub. L. 111–203, title X, §1084(1), July 21, 2010, 124 Stat. 2081.)

EDITORIAL NOTES

AMENDMENTS

2010—Subsec. (b). Pub. L. 111–203 substituted "Bureau" for "Board".

STATUTORY NOTES AND RELATED SUBSIDIARIES

EFFECTIVE DATE OF 2010 AMENDMENT

Amendment by Pub. L. 111–203 effective on the designated transfer date, see section 1100H of Pub. L. 111–203, set out as a note under section 552a of Title 5, Government Organization and Employees.

§1693e. Preauthorized transfers

(a) A preauthorized electronic fund transfer from a consumer's account may be authorized by the consumer only in writing, and a copy of such authorization shall be provided to the consumer when made. A consumer may stop payment of a preauthorized electronic fund transfer by notifying the financial institution orally or in writing at any time up to three business days preceding the scheduled date of such transfer. The financial institution may require written confirmation to be provided to it within fourteen days of an oral notification if, when the oral notification is made, the consumer is advised of such requirement and the address to which such confirmation should be sent.

(b) In the case of preauthorized transfers from a consumer's account to the same person which may vary in amount, the financial institution or designated payee shall, prior to each transfer, provide reasonable advance notice to the consumer, in accordance with regulations of the Bureau, of the amount to be transferred and the scheduled date of the transfer.

(Pub. L. 90–321, title IX, §907, as added Pub. L. 95–630, title XX, §2001, Nov. 10, 1978, 92 Stat. 3733; amended Pub. L. 111–203, title X, §1084(1), July 21, 2010, 124 Stat. 2081.)

AMENDMENTS

2010—Subsec. (b). Pub. L. 111–203 substituted "Bureau" for "Board".

STATUTORY NOTES AND RELATED SUBSIDIARIES

EFFECTIVE DATE OF 2010 AMENDMENT

Amendment by Pub. L. 111–203 effective on the designated transfer date, see section 1100H of Pub. L. 111–203, set out as a note under section 552a of Title 5, Government Organization and Employees.

§1693f. Error resolution

(a) Notification to financial institution of error

If a financial institution, within sixty days after having transmitted to a consumer documentation pursuant to section 1693d(a), (c), or (d) of this title or notification pursuant to section 1693d(b) of this title, receives oral or written notice in which the consumer—

(1) sets forth or otherwise enables the financial institution to identify the name and account number of the consumer;

(2) indicates the consumer's belief that the documentation, or, in the case of notification pursuant to section 1693d(b) of this title, the consumer's account, contains an error and the amount of such error; and

(3) sets forth the reasons for the consumer's belief (where applicable) that an error has occurred,

the financial institution shall investigate the alleged error, determine whether an error has occurred, and report or mail the results of such investigation and determination to the consumer within ten business days. The financial institution may require written confirmation to be provided to it within ten business days of an oral notification of error if, when the oral notification is made, the consumer is advised of such requirement and the address to which such confirmation should be sent. A financial institution which requires written confirmation in accordance with the previous sentence need not provisionally recredit a consumer's account in accordance with subsection (c), nor shall the financial institution be liable under subsection (e) if the written confirmation is not received within the ten-day period referred to in the previous sentence.

(b) Correction of error; interest

If the financial institution determines that an error did occur, it shall promptly, but in no event more than one business day after such determination, correct the error, subject to section 1693g of this title, including the crediting of interest where applicable.

(c) Provisional recredit of consumer's account

If a financial institution receives notice of an error in the manner and within the time period specified in subsection (a), it may, in lieu of the requirements of subsections (a) and (b), within ten business days after receiving such notice provisionally recredit the consumer's account for the amount alleged to be in error, subject to section 1693g of this title, including interest where applicable, pending the conclusion of its investigation and its determination of whether an error has occurred. Such investigation shall be concluded not later than forty-five days after receipt of notice of the error. During the pendency of the investigation, the consumer shall have full use of the funds provisionally recredited.

(d) Absence of error; finding; explanation

If the financial institution determines after its investigation pursuant to subsection (a) or (c) that an error did not occur, it shall deliver or mail to the consumer an explanation of its findings within 3 business days after the conclusion of its investigation, and upon request of the consumer promptly deliver or mail to the consumer reproductions of all documents which the financial institution relied on to conclude that such error did not occur. The financial institution shall include notice of the right to request reproductions with the explanation of its findings.

(e) Treble damages

If in any action under section 1693m [1] of this title, the court finds that—

(1) the financial institution did not provisionally recredit a consumer's account within the ten-day period specified in subsection (c), and the financial institution (A) did not make a good faith investigation of the alleged error, or (B) did not have a reasonable basis for believing that the consumer's account was not in error; or

(2) the financial institution knowingly and willfully concluded that the consumer's account was not in error when such conclusion could not reasonably have been drawn from the evidence available to the financial institution at the time of its investigation,

then the consumer shall be entitled to treble damages determined under section 1693m(a)(1) [1] of this title.

(f) Acts constituting error

For the purpose of this section, an error consists of—

(1) an unauthorized electronic fund transfer;

(2) an incorrect electronic fund transfer from or to the consumer's account;

(3) the omission from a periodic statement of an electronic fund transfer affecting the consumer's account which should have been included;

(4) a computational error by the financial institution;

(5) the consumer's receipt of an incorrect amount of money from an electronic terminal;

(6) a consumer's request for additional information or clarification concerning an electronic fund transfer or any documentation required by this subchapter; or

(7) any other error described in regulations of the Bureau.

(Pub. L. 90–321, title IX, §908, as added Pub. L. 95–630, title XX, §2001, Nov. 10, 1978, 92 Stat. 3733; amended Pub. L. 111–203, title X, §1084(1), July 21, 2010, 124 Stat. 2081.)

EDITORIAL NOTES

REFERENCES IN TEXT

Section 1693m of this title, referred to in subsec. (e), was in the original a reference to section 915 of Pub. L. 90–321, and was translated as meaning section 916 of Pub. L. 90–321 to reflect the probable intent of Congress and the renumbering of section 915 of Pub. L. 90–321 as section 916 by Pub. L. 111–24, title IV, §401(1), May 22, 2009, 123 Stat. 1751.

AMENDMENTS

2010—Subsec. (f)(7). Pub. L. 111–203 substituted "Bureau" for "Board".

STATUTORY NOTES AND RELATED SUBSIDIARIES

EFFECTIVE DATE OF 2010 AMENDMENT

Amendment by Pub. L. 111–203 effective on the designated transfer date, see section 1100H of Pub. L. 111–203, set out as a note under section 552a of Title 5, Government Organization and Employees.

[1] See References in Text note below.

§1693g. Consumer liability

(a) Unauthorized electronic fund transfers; limit

A consumer shall be liable for any unauthorized electronic fund transfer involving the account of such consumer only if the card or other means of access utilized for such transfer was an accepted card or other meanas [1] of access and if the issuer of such card, code, or other means of access has provided a means whereby the user of such card, code, or other means of access can be identified as the person authorized to use it, such as by signature, photograph, or fingerprint or by electronic or mechanical confirmation. In no event, however, shall a consumer's liability for an unauthorized transfer exceed the lesser of—

(1) $50; or

(2) the amount of money or value of property or services obtained in such unauthorized electronic fund transfer prior to the time the financial institution is notified of, or otherwise becomes aware of, circumstances which lead to the reasonable belief that an unauthorized electronic fund transfer involving the consumer's account has been or may be effected. Notice under this paragraph is sufficient when such steps have been taken as may be reasonably required in the ordinary course of business to provide the financial institution with the pertinent information, whether or not any particular officer, employee, or agent of the financial institution does in fact receive such information.

Notwithstanding the foregoing, reimbursement need not be made to the consumer for losses the financial institution establishes would not have occurred but for the failure of the consumer to report within sixty days of transmittal of the statement (or in extenuating circumstances such as extended travel or hospitalization, within a reasonable time under the circumstances) any unauthorized electronic fund transfer or account error which appears on the periodic statement provided to the consumer under section 1693d of this title. In addition, reimbursement need not be made to the consumer for losses which the financial institution establishes would not have occurred but for the failure of the consumer to report any loss or theft of a card or other means of access within two business days after the consumer learns of the loss or theft (or in extenuating circumstances such as extended travel or hospitalization, within a longer period which is reasonable under the circumstances), but the consumer's liability under this subsection in any such case may not exceed a total of $500, or the amount of unauthorized electronic fund transfers which occur following the close of two business days (or such longer period) after the consumer learns of the loss or theft but prior to notice to the financial institution under this subsection, whichever is less.

(b) Burden of proof

In any action which involves a consumer's liability for an unauthorized electronic fund transfer, the burden of proof is upon the financial institution to show that the electronic fund transfer was authorized or, if the electronic fund transfer was unauthorized, then the burden of proof is upon the financial institution to establish that the conditions of liability set forth in subsection (a) have been met, and, if the transfer was initiated after the effective date of section 1693c of this title, that the disclosures required to be made to the consumer under section 1693c(a)(1) and (2) of this title were in fact made in accordance with such section.

(c) Determination of limitation on liability

In the event of a transaction which involves both an unauthorized electronic fund transfer and an extension of credit as defined in section 1602(e) [2] of this title pursuant to an agreement between the consumer and the financial institution to extend such credit to the consumer in the event the consumer's account is overdrawn, the limitation on the consumer's liability for such transaction shall be determined solely in accordance with this section.

(d) Restriction on liability

Nothing in this section imposes liability upon a consumer for an unauthorized electronic fund transfer in excess of his liability for such a transfer under other applicable law or under any agreement with the consumer's financial institution.

(e) Scope of liability

Except as provided in this section, a consumer incurs no liability from an unauthorized electronic fund transfer.

(Pub. L. 90–321, title IX, §909, as added Pub. L. 95–630, title XX, §2001, Nov. 10, 1978, 92 Stat. 3734.)

EDITORIAL NOTES

REFERENCES IN TEXT

Section 1602(e) of this title, referred to in subsec. (c), was redesignated section 1602(f) of this title by Pub. L. 111–203, title X, §1100A(1)(A), July 21, 2010, 124 Stat. 2107.

[1] So in original. Probably should be "means".

[2] See References in Text note below.

§1693h. Liability of financial institutions

(a) Action or failure to act proximately causing damages

Subject to subsections (b) and (c), a financial institution shall be liable to a consumer for all damages proximately caused by—

(1) the financial institution's failure to make an electronic fund transfer, in accordance with the terms and conditions of an account, in the correct amount or in a timely manner when properly instructed to do so by the consumer, except where—

(A) the consumer's account has insufficient funds;

(B) the funds are subject to legal process or other encumbrance restricting such transfer;

(C) such transfer would exceed an established credit limit;

(D) an electronic terminal has insufficient cash to complete the transaction; or

(E) as otherwise provided in regulations of the Bureau;

(2) the financial institution's failure to make an electronic fund transfer due to insufficient funds when the financial [1] institution failed to credit, in accordance with the terms and conditions of an account, a deposit of funds to the consumer's account which would have provided sufficient funds to make the transfer, and

(3) the financial institution's failure to stop payment of a preauthorized transfer from a consumer's account when instructed to do so in accordance with the terms and conditions of the account.

(b) Acts of God and technical malfunctions

A financial institution shall not be liable under subsection (a)(1) or (2) if the financial institution shows by a preponderance of the evidence that its action or failure to act resulted from—

(1) an act of God or other circumstance beyond its control, that it exercised reasonable care to prevent such an occurrence, and that it exercised such diligence as the circumstances required; or

(2) a technical malfunction which was known to the consumer at the time he attempted to initiate an electronic fund transfer or, in the case of a preauthorized transfer, at the time such transfer should have occurred.

(c) Intent

In the case of a failure described in subsection (a) which was not intentional and which resulted from a bona fide error, notwithstanding the maintenance of procedures reasonably adapted to avoid any such error, the financial institution shall be liable for actual damages proved.

(d) Exception for damaged notices

If the notice required to be posted pursuant to section 1693b(d)(3)(B)(i) of this title by an automated teller machine operator has been posted by such operator in compliance with such section and the notice is subsequently removed, damaged, or altered by any person other than the operator of the automated teller machine, the operator shall have no liability under this section for failure to comply with section 1693b(d)(3)(B)(i) of this title.

(Pub. L. 90–321, title IX, §910, as added Pub. L. 95–630, title XX, §2001, Nov. 10, 1978, 92 Stat. 3735; amended Pub. L. 106–102, title VII, §705, Nov. 12, 1999, 113 Stat. 1465; Pub. L. 111–203, title X, §1084(1), July 21, 2010, 124 Stat. 2081.)

EDITORIAL NOTES

AMENDMENTS

2010—Subsec. (a)(1)(E). Pub. L. 111–203 substituted "Bureau" for "Board".
1999—Subsec. (d). Pub. L. 106–102 added subsec. (d).

STATUTORY NOTES AND RELATED SUBSIDIARIES

EFFECTIVE DATE OF 2010 AMENDMENT

Amendment by Pub. L. 111–203 effective on the designated transfer date, see section 1100H of Pub. L. 111–203, set out as a note under section 552a of Title 5, Government Organization and Employees.

1 So in original. Probably should be "financial".

§1693i. Issuance of cards or other means of access

(a) Prohibition; proper issuance

No person may issue to a consumer any card, code, or other means of access to such consumer's account for the purpose of initiating an electronic fund transfer other than—

(1) in response to a request or application therefor; or

(2) as a renewal of, or in substitution for, an accepted card, code, or other means of access, whether issued by the initial issuer or a successor.

(b) Exceptions

Notwithstanding the provisions of subsection (a), a person may distribute to a consumer on an unsolicited basis a card, code, or other means of access for use in initiating an electronic fund transfer from such consumer's account, if—

(1) such card, code, or other means of access is not validated;

(2) such distribution is accompanied by a complete disclosure, in accordance with section 1693c of this title, of the consumer's rights and liabilities which will apply if such card, code, or other means of access is validated;

(3) such distribution is accompanied by a clear explanation, in accordance with regulations of the Bureau, that such card, code, or other means of access is not validated and how the consumer may dispose of such code, card, or other means of access if validation is not desired; and

(4) such card, code, or other means of access is validated only in response to a request or application from the consumer, upon verification of the consumer's identity.

(c) Validation

For the purpose of subsection (b), a card, code, or other means of access is validated when it may be used to initiate an electronic fund transfer.

(Pub. L. 90–321, title IX, §911, as added Pub. L. 95–630, title XX, §2001, Nov. 10, 1978, 92 Stat. 3736; amended Pub. L. 111–203, title X, §1084(1), July 21, 2010, 124 Stat. 2081.)

AMENDMENTS

2010—Subsec. (b)(3). Pub. L. 111–203 substituted "Bureau" for "Board".

STATUTORY NOTES AND RELATED SUBSIDIARIES

EFFECTIVE DATE OF 2010 AMENDMENT

Amendment by Pub. L. 111–203 effective on the designated transfer date, see section 1100H of Pub. L. 111–203, set out as a note under section 552a of Title 5, Government Organization and Employees.

§1693j. Suspension of obligations

If a system malfunction prevents the effectuation of an electronic fund transfer initiated by a consumer to another person, and such other person has agreed to accept payment by such means, the consumer's obligation to the other person shall be suspended until the malfunction is corrected and the electronic fund transfer may be completed, unless such other person has subsequently, by written request, demanded payment by means other than an electronic fund transfer.

(Pub. L. 90–321, title IX, §912, as added Pub. L. 95–630, title XX, §2001, Nov. 10, 1978, 92 Stat. 3737.)

§1693k. Compulsory use of electronic fund transfers

No person may—

(1) condition the extension of credit to a consumer on such consumer's repayment by means of preauthorized electronic fund transfers; or

(2) require a consumer to establish an account for receipt of electronic fund transfers with a particular financial institution as a condition of employment or receipt of a government benefit.

(Pub. L. 90–321, title IX, §913, as added Pub. L. 95–630, title XX, §2001, Nov. 10, 1978, 92 Stat. 3737.)

§1693l. Waiver of rights

No writing or other agreement between a consumer and any other person may contain any provision which constitutes a waiver of any right conferred or cause of action created by this subchapter. Nothing in this section prohibits, however, any writing or other agreement which grants to a consumer a more extensive right or remedy or greater protection than contained in this subchapter or a waiver given in settlement of a dispute or action.

(Pub. L. 90–321, title IX, §914, as added Pub. L. 95–630, title XX, §2001, Nov. 10, 1978, 92 Stat. 3737.)

§1693l–1. General-use prepaid cards, gift certificates, and store gift cards

(a) Definitions

In this section, the following definitions shall apply:

(1) Dormancy fee; inactivity charge or fee

The terms "dormancy fee" and "inactivity charge or fee" mean a fee, charge, or penalty for non-use or inactivity of a gift certificate, store gift card, or general-use prepaid card.

(2) General use [1] prepaid card, gift certificate, and store gift card

(A) General-use prepaid card

The term "general-use prepaid card" means a card or other payment code or device issued by any person that is—

(i) redeemable at multiple, unaffiliated merchants or service providers, or automated teller machines;

(ii) issued in a requested amount, whether or not that amount may, at the option of the issuer, be increased in value or reloaded if requested by the holder;

(iii) purchased or loaded on a prepaid basis; and

(iv) honored, upon presentation, by merchants for goods or services, or at automated teller machines.

(B) Gift certificate

The term "gift certificate" means an electronic promise that is—

(i) redeemable at a single merchant or an affiliated group of merchants that share the same name, mark, or logo;

(ii) issued in a specified amount that may not be increased or reloaded;

(iii) purchased on a prepaid basis in exchange for payment; and

(iv) honored upon presentation by such single merchant or affiliated group of merchants for goods or services.

(C) Store gift card

The term "store gift card" means an electronic promise, plastic card, or other payment code or device that is—

(i) redeemable at a single merchant or an affiliated group of merchants that share the same name, mark, or logo;

(ii) issued in a specified amount, whether or not that amount may be increased in value or reloaded at the request of the holder;

(iii) purchased on a prepaid basis in exchange for payment; and

(iv) honored upon presentation by such single merchant or affiliated group of merchants for goods or services.

(D) Exclusions

The terms "general-use prepaid card", "gift certificate", and "store gift card" do not include an electronic promise, plastic card, or payment code or device that is—

(i) used solely for telephone services;

(ii) reloadable and not marketed or labeled as a gift card or gift certificate;

(iii) a loyalty, award, or promotional gift card, as defined by the Bureau;

(iv) not marketed to the general public;

(v) issued in paper form only (including for tickets and events); or

(vi) redeemable solely for admission to events or venues at a particular location or group of affiliated locations, which may also include services or goods obtainable—

(I) at the event or venue after admission; or

(II) in conjunction with admission to such events or venues, at specific locations affiliated with and in geographic proximity to the event or venue.

(3) Service fee

(A) In general

The term "service fee" means a periodic fee, charge, or penalty for holding or use of a gift certificate, store gift card, or general-use prepaid card.

(B) Exclusion

With respect to a general-use prepaid card, the term "service fee" does not include a one-time initial issuance fee.

(b) Prohibition on imposition of fees or charges

(1) In general

Except as provided under paragraphs (2) through (4), it shall be unlawful for any person to impose a dormancy fee, an inactivity charge or fee, or a service fee with respect to a gift certificate, store gift card, or general-use prepaid card.

(2) Exceptions

A dormancy fee, inactivity charge or fee, or service fee may be charged with respect to a gift certificate, store gift card, or general-use prepaid card, if—

(A) there has been no activity with respect to the certificate or card in the 12-month period ending on the date on which the charge or fee is imposed;

(B) the disclosure requirements of paragraph (3) have been met;

(C) not more than one fee may be charged in any given month; and

(D) any additional requirements that the Bureau may establish through rulemaking under subsection (d) have been met.

(3) Disclosure requirements

The disclosure requirements of this paragraph are met if—

(A) the gift certificate, store gift card, or general-use prepaid card clearly and conspicuously states—

(i) that a dormancy fee, inactivity charge or fee, or service fee may be charged;

(ii) the amount of such fee or charge;

(iii) how often such fee or charge may be assessed; and

(iv) that such fee or charge may be assessed for inactivity; and

(B) the issuer or vendor of such certificate or card informs the purchaser of such charge or fee before such certificate or card is purchased, regardless of whether the certificate or card is purchased in person, over the Internet, or by telephone.

(4) Exclusion

The prohibition under paragraph (1) shall not apply to any gift certificate—
  (A) that is distributed pursuant to an award, loyalty, or promotional program, as defined by the Bureau; and
  (B) with respect to which, there is no money or other value exchanged.

(c) Prohibition on sale of gift cards with expiration dates

(1) In general

Except as provided under paragraph (2), it shall be unlawful for any person to sell or issue a gift certificate, store gift card, or general-use prepaid card that is subject to an expiration date.

(2) Exceptions

A gift certificate, store gift card, or general-use prepaid card may contain an expiration date if—
  (A) the expiration date is not earlier than 5 years after the date on which the gift certificate was issued, or the date on which card funds were last loaded to a store gift card or general-use prepaid card; and
  (B) the terms of expiration are clearly and conspicuously stated.

(d) Additional rulemaking

(1) In general

The Bureau shall—
  (A) prescribe regulations to carry out this section, in addition to any other rules or regulations required by this subchapter, including such additional requirements as appropriate relating to the amount of dormancy fees, inactivity charges or fees, or service fees that may be assessed and the amount of remaining value of a gift certificate, store gift card, or general-use prepaid card below which such charges or fees may be assessed; and
  (B) shall ^{2} determine the extent to which the individual definitions and provisions of this subchapter or Regulation E should apply to general-use prepaid cards, gift certificates, and store gift cards.

(2) Consultation

In prescribing regulations under this subsection, the Bureau shall consult with the Federal Trade Commission.

(3) Timing; effective date

The regulations required by this subsection shall be issued in final form not later than 9 months after May 22, 2009.

(Pub. L. 90–321, title IX, §915, as added Pub. L. 111–24, title IV, §401(2), May 22, 2009, 123 Stat. 1751; amended Pub. L. 111–203, title X, §1084(1), July 21, 2010, 124 Stat. 2081.)

EDITORIAL NOTES

PRIOR PROVISIONS

A prior section 915 of Pub. L. 90–321 was renumbered section 916 and is classified to section 1693m of this title.

AMENDMENTS

2010—Pub. L. 111–203 substituted "Bureau" for "Board" wherever appearing.

STATUTORY NOTES AND RELATED SUBSIDIARIES

EFFECTIVE DATE OF 2010 AMENDMENT

Amendment by Pub. L. 111–203 effective on the designated transfer date, see section 1100H of Pub. L. 111–203, set out as a note under section 552a of Title 5, Government Organization and Employees.

EFFECTIVE DATE

Pub. L. 111–24, title IV, §403, as added by Pub. L. 111–209, §1, July 27, 2010, 124 Stat. 2254, provided that:
"(a) IN GENERAL.—Except as provided under subsection (b) of this section, this title [enacting this section and amending sections 1693m to 1693r of this title and provisions set out as a note under section 1693 of this title] and the amendments made by this title shall become effective 15 months after the date of enactment of this Act [May 22, 2009].
"(b) EXCEPTION.—
  "(1) IN GENERAL.—In the case of a gift certificate, store gift card, or general-use prepaid card that was produced prior to April 1, 2010, the effective date of the disclosure requirements described in sections 915(b)(3) and (c)(2)(B) of the Electronic Funds [probably should be "Fund"] Transfer Act [15 U.S.C. 1693l–1(b)(3), (c)(2)(B)] shall be January 31, 2011, provided that an issuer of such a certificate or card shall—

"(A) comply with paragraphs (1) and (2) of section 915(b) of such Act [15 U.S.C. 1693l–1(b)(1), (2)];[1]

"(B) consider any such certificate or card for which funds expire to have no expiration date with respect to the underlying funds;

"(C) at a consumer's request, replace such certificate or card that has funds remaining at no cost to the consumer; and

"(D) comply with the disclosure requirements of paragraph (2) of this subsection.

"(2) DISCLOSURE REQUIREMENTS.—The disclosure requirements of this subsection are met by providing notice to consumers, via in-store signage, messages during customer service calls, Web sites, and general advertising, that—

"(A) any such certificate or card for which funds expire shall be deemed to have no expiration date with respect to the underlying funds;

"(B) consumers holding such certificate or card shall have a right to a free replacement certificate or card that includes the packaging and materials, typically associated with such a certificate or card; and

"(C) any dormancy fee, inactivity fee, or service fee for such certificates or cards that might otherwise be charged shall not be charged if such fees do not comply with section 915 of the Electronic Funds [probably should be "Fund"] Transfer Act [15 U.S.C. 1693l–1].

"(3) PERIOD FOR DISCLOSURE REQUIREMENTS.—The notice requirements in paragraph (2) of this subsection shall continue until January 31, 2013."

Pub. L. 111–24, title IV, §403, May 22, 2009, 123 Stat. 1754, which provided that title IV of Pub. L. 111–24 was to become effective 15 months after May 22, 2009, was repealed by Pub. L. 111–209, §1, July 27, 2010, 124 Stat. 2254.

[1] So in original. Probably should be "General-use".

[2] So in original. The word "shall" probably should not appear.

§1693m. Civil liability

(a) Individual or class action for damages; amount of award

Except as otherwise provided by this section and section 1693h of this title, any person who fails to comply with any provision of this subchapter with respect to any consumer, except for an error resolved in accordance with section 1693f of this title, is liable to such consumer in an amount equal to the sum of—

(1) any actual damage sustained by such consumer as a result of such failure;

(2)(A) in the case of an individual action, an amount not less than $100 nor greater than $1,000; or

(B) in the case of a class action, such amount as the court may allow, except that (i) as to each member of the class no minimum recovery shall be applicable, and (ii) the total recovery under this subparagraph in any class action or series of class actions arising out of the same failure to comply by the same person shall not be more than the lesser of $500,000 or 1 per centum of the net worth of the defendant; and

(3) in the case of any successful action to enforce the foregoing liability, the costs of the action, together with a reasonable attorney's fee as determined by the court.

(b) Factors determining amount of award

In determining the amount of liability in any action under subsection (a), the court shall consider, among other relevant factors—

(1) in any individual action under subsection (a)(2)(A), the frequency and persistence of noncompliance, the nature of such noncompliance, and the extent to which the noncompliance was intentional; or

(2) in any class action under subsection (a)(2)(B), the frequency and persistence of noncompliance, the nature of such noncompliance, the resources of the defendant, the number of persons adversely affected, and the extent to which the noncompliance was intentional.

(c) Unintentional violations; bona fide error

Except as provided in section 1693h of this title, a person may not be held liable in any action brought under this section for a violation of this subchapter if the person shows by a preponderance of evidence that the violation was not intentional and resulted from a bona fide error notwithstanding the maintenance of procedures reasonably adapted to avoid any such error.

(d) Good faith compliance with rule, regulation, or interpretation

No provision of this section or section 1693n [1] of this title imposing any liability shall apply to—

(1) any act done or omitted in good faith in conformity with any rule, regulation, or interpretation thereof by the Bureau or the Board or in conformity with any interpretation or approval by an official or employee of the Bureau of

Consumer Financial Protection or the Federal Reserve System duly authorized by the Bureau or the Board to issue such interpretations or approvals under such procedures as the Bureau or the Board may prescribe therefor; or

(2) any failure to make disclosure in proper form if a financial institution utilized an appropriate model clause issued by the Bureau or the Board,

notwithstanding that after such act, omission, or failure has occurred, such rule, regulation, approval, or model clause is amended, rescinded, or determined by judicial or other authority to be invalid for any reason.

(e) Notification to consumer prior to action; adjustment of consumer's account

A person has no liability under this section for any failure to comply with any requirement under this subchapter if, prior to the institution of an action under this section, the person notifies the consumer concerned of the failure, complies with the requirements of this subchapter, and makes an appropriate adjustment to the consumer's account and pays actual damages or, where applicable, damages in accordance with section 1693h of this title.

(f) Action in bad faith or for harassment; attorney's fees

On a finding by the court that an unsuccessful action under this section was brought in bad faith or for purposes of harassment, the court shall award to the defendant attorney's fees reasonable in relation to the work expended and costs.

(g) Jurisdiction of courts; time for maintenance of action

Without regard to the amount in controversy, any action under this section may be brought in any United States district court, or in any other court of competent jurisdiction, within one year from the date of the occurrence of the violation.

(Pub. L. 90–321, title IX, §916, formerly §915, as added Pub. L. 95–630, title XX, §2001, Nov. 10, 1978, 92 Stat. 3737; renumbered §916, Pub. L. 111–24, title IV, §401(1), May 22, 2009, 123 Stat. 1751; amended Pub. L. 111–203, title X, §1084(1), (4), July 21, 2010, 124 Stat. 2081, 2082.)

EDITORIAL NOTES

REFERENCES IN TEXT

Section 1693n of this title, referred to in subsec. (d), was in the original a reference to section 916 of Pub. L. 90–321, and was translated as meaning section 917 of Pub. L. 90–321 to reflect the probable intent of Congress and the renumbering of section 916 of Pub. L. 90–321 as section 917 by Pub. L. 111–24, title IV, §401(1), May 22, 2009, 123 Stat. 1751.

PRIOR PROVISIONS

A prior section 916 of Pub. L. 90–321 was renumbered section 917 and is classified to section 1693n of this title.

AMENDMENTS

2010—Pub. L. 111–203, §1084(1), which directed the substitution of "Bureau" for "Board" wherever appearing in section, was not executed in subsec. (d), which was the only place such term appeared, to reflect the probable intent of Congress and the amendment by Pub. L. 111–203, §1084(4). See below.

Subsec. (d). Pub. L. 111–203, §1084(4), struck out "of Board or approval of duly authorized official or employee of Federal Reserve System" after "interpretation" in heading that had been supplied editorially and inserted "Bureau of Consumer Financial Protection or the" before "Federal Reserve System" in par. (1) and "Bureau or the" before "Board" wherever appearing.

STATUTORY NOTES AND RELATED SUBSIDIARIES

EFFECTIVE DATE OF 2010 AMENDMENT

Amendment by Pub. L. 111–203 effective on the designated transfer date, see section 1100H of Pub. L. 111–203, set out as a note under section 552a of Title 5, Government Organization and Employees.

---

[1] See References in Text note below.

§1693n. Criminal liability

(a) Violations respecting giving of false or inaccurate information, failure to provide information, and failure to comply with provisions of this subchapter

Whoever knowingly and willfully—

 (1) gives false or inaccurate information or fails to provide information which he is required to disclose by this subchapter or any regulation issued thereunder; or

 (2) otherwise fails to comply with any provision of this subchapter;

shall be fined not more than $5,000 or imprisoned not more than one year, or both.

(b) Violations affecting interstate or foreign commerce

Whoever—

 (1) knowingly, in a transaction affecting interstate or foreign commerce, uses or attempts or conspires to use any counterfeit, fictitious, altered, forged, lost, stolen, or fraudulently obtained debit instrument to obtain money, goods, services, or anything else of value which within any one-year period has a value aggregating $1,000 or more; or

 (2) with unlawful or fraudulent intent, transports or attempts or conspires to transport in interstate or foreign commerce a counterfeit, fictitious, altered, forged, lost, stolen, or fraudulently obtained debit instrument knowing the same to be counterfeit, fictitious, altered, forged, lost, stolen, or fraudulently obtained; or

 (3) with unlawful or fraudulent intent, uses any instrumentality of interstate or foreign commerce to sell or transport a counterfeit, fictitious, altered, forged, lost, stolen, or fraudulently obtained debit instrument knowing the same to be counterfeit, fictitious, altered, forged, lost, stolen, or fraudulently obtained; or

 (4) knowingly receives, conceals, uses, or transports money, goods, services, or anything else of value (except tickets for interstate or foreign transportation) which (A) within any one-year period has a value aggregating $1,000 or more, (B) has moved in or is part of, or which constitutes interstate or foreign commerce, and (C) has been obtained with a counterfeit, fictitious, altered, forged, lost, stolen, or fraudulently obtained debit instrument; or

 (5) knowingly receives, conceals, uses, sells, or transports in interstate or foreign commerce one or more tickets for interstate or foreign transportation, which (A) within any one-year period have a value aggregating $500 or more, and (B) have been purchased or obtained with one or more counterfeit, fictitious, altered, forged, lost, stolen, or fraudulently obtained debit instrument; or

 (6) in a transaction affecting interstate or foreign commerce, furnishes money, property, services, or anything else of value, which within any one-year period has a value aggregating $1,000 or more, through the use of any counterfeit, fictitious, altered, forged, lost, stolen, or fraudulently obtained debit instrument knowing the same to be counterfeit, fictitious, altered, forged, lost, stolen, or fraudulently obtained—

shall be fined not more than $10,000 or imprisoned not more than ten years, or both.

(c) "Debit instrument" defined

As used in this section, the term "debit instrument" means a card, code, or other device, other than a check, draft, or similar paper instrument, by the use of which a person may initiate an electronic fund transfer.

(Pub. L. 90–321, title IX, §917, formerly §916, as added Pub. L. 95–630, title XX, §2001, Nov. 10, 1978, 92 Stat. 3738; renumbered §917, Pub. L. 111–24, title IV, §401(1), May 22, 2009, 123 Stat. 1751.)

EDITORIAL NOTES

PRIOR PROVISIONS

A prior section 917 of Pub. L. 90–321 was renumbered section 918 and is classified to section 1693o of this title.

§1693o. Administrative enforcement

(a) Enforcing agencies

Subject to subtitle B of the Consumer Financial Protection Act of 2010 [12 U.S.C. 5511 et seq.], compliance with the requirements imposed under this subchapter shall be enforced under—

 (1) section 8 of the Federal Deposit Insurance Act [12 U.S.C. 1818], by the appropriate Federal banking agency, as defined in section 3(q) of the Federal Deposit Insurance Act (12 U.S.C. 1813(q)), with respect to—

  (A) national banks, Federal savings associations, and Federal branches and Federal agencies of foreign banks;

  (B) member banks of the Federal Reserve System (other than national banks), branches and agencies of foreign banks (other than Federal branches, Federal agencies, and insured State branches of foreign banks), commercial lending companies owned or controlled by foreign banks, and organizations operating under section 25 or 25A of the Federal Reserve Act [12 U.S.C. 601 et seq., 611 et seq.]; and

  (C) banks and State savings associations insured by the Federal Deposit Insurance Corporation (other than members of the Federal Reserve System), and insured State branches of foreign banks;

 (2) the Federal Credit Union Act [12 U.S.C. 1751 et seq.], by the Administrator of the National Credit Union Administration with respect to any Federal credit union;

(3) part A of subtitle VII of title 49, by the Secretary of Transportation, with respect to any air carrier or foreign air carrier subject to that part;

(4) the Securities Exchange Act of 1934 [15 U.S.C. 78a et seq.], by the Securities and Exchange Commission, with respect to any broker or dealer subject to that Act and [1]

(5) subtitle E of the Consumer Financial Protection Act of 2010 [12 U.S.C. 5561 et seq.], by the Bureau, with respect to any person subject to this subchapter, except that the Bureau shall not have authority to enforce the requirements of section 1693o–2 of this title or any regulations prescribed by the Board under section 1693o–2 of this title.

The terms used in paragraph (1) that are not defined in this subchapter or otherwise defined in section 3(s) of the Federal Deposit Insurance Act (12 U.S.C. 1813(s)) shall have the meaning given to them in section 1(b) of the International Banking Act of 1978 (12 U.S.C. 3101).

(b) Violations of subchapter deemed violations of pre-existing statutory requirements; additional powers

For the purpose of the exercise by any agency referred to in any of paragraphs (1) through (4) of subsection (a) of its powers under any Act referred to in that subsection, a violation of any requirement imposed under this subchapter shall be deemed to be a violation of a requirement imposed under that Act. In addition to its powers under any provision of law specifically referred to in any of paragraphs (1) through (4) of subsection (a), each of the agencies referred to in that subsection may exercise, for the purpose of enforcing compliance with any requirement imposed under this subchapter, any other authority conferred on it by law.

(c) Overall enforcement authority of the Federal Trade Commission

Except to the extent that enforcement of the requirements imposed under this subchapter is specifically committed to some other Government agency under any of paragraphs (1) through (4) of subsection (a), and subject to subtitle B of the Consumer Financial Protection Act of 2010, the Federal Trade Commission shall be authorized to enforce such requirements. For the purpose of the exercise by the Federal Trade Commission of its functions and powers under the Federal Trade Commission Act [15 U.S.C. 41 et seq.], a violation of any requirement imposed under this subchapter shall be deemed a violation of a requirement imposed under that Act. All of the functions and powers of the Federal Trade Commission under the Federal Trade Commission Act are available to the Federal Trade Commission to enforce compliance by any person subject to the jurisdiction of the Federal Trade Commission with the requirements imposed under this subchapter, irrespective of whether that person is engaged in commerce or meets any other jurisdictional tests under the Federal Trade Commission Act.

(Pub. L. 90–321, title IX, §918, formerly §917, as added Pub. L. 95–630, title XX, §2001, Nov. 10, 1978, 92 Stat. 3739; amended Pub. L. 101–73, title VII, §744(o), Aug. 9, 1989, 103 Stat. 440; Pub. L. 102–242, title II, §212(f), Dec. 19, 1991, 105 Stat. 2301; Pub. L. 104–287, §6(h), Oct. 11, 1996, 110 Stat. 3399; renumbered §918, Pub. L. 111–24, title IV, §401(1), May 22, 2009, 123 Stat. 1751; Pub. L. 111–203, title X, §1084(5), July 21, 2010, 124 Stat. 2082.)

EDITORIAL NOTES

REFERENCES IN TEXT

The Consumer Financial Protection Act of 2010, referred to in subsecs. (a) and (c), is title X of Pub. L. 111–203, July 21, 2010, 124 Stat. 1955. Subtitles B (§§1021–1029A) and E (§§1051–1058) of the Act are classified generally to parts B (§5511 et seq.) and E (§5561 et seq.), respectively, of subchapter V of chapter 53 of Title 12, Banks and Banking. For complete classification of subtitles B and E to the Code, see Tables.

Sections 25 and 25A of the Federal Reserve Act, referred to in subsec. (a)(1)(B), are classified to subchapters I (§601 et seq.) and II (§611 et seq.), respectively, of chapter 6 of Title 12, Banks and Banking.

The Federal Credit Union Act, referred to in subsec. (a)(2), is act June 26, 1934, ch. 750, 48 Stat. 1216, which is classified generally to chapter 14 (§1751 et seq.) of Title 12. For complete classification of this Act to the Code, see section 1751 of Title 12 and Tables.

The Securities Exchange Act of 1934, referred to in subsec. (a)(4), is act June 6, 1934, ch. 404, 48 Stat. 881, which is classified principally to chapter 2B (§78a et seq.) of this title. For complete classification of this Act to the Code, see section 78a of this title and Tables.

The Federal Trade Commission Act, referred to in subsec. (c), is act Sept. 26, 1914, ch. 311, 38 Stat. 717, which is classified generally to subchapter I (§41 et seq.) of chapter 2 of this title. For complete classification of this Act to the Code, see section 58 of this title and Tables.

CODIFICATION

In subsec. (a)(3), "part A of subtitle VII of title 49" substituted for "the Federal Aviation Act of 1958 [49 App. U.S.C. 1301 et seq.]" and "that part" substituted for "that Act" on authority of Pub. L. 103–272, §6(b), July 5, 1994, 108 Stat. 1378, the first section of which enacted subtitles II, III, and V to X of Title 49, Transportation.

A prior section 918 of Pub. L. 90–321 was renumbered section 921 and is classified to section 1693p of this title.

AMENDMENTS

2010—Subsec. (a). Pub. L. 111–203, §1084(5)(A)(i), substituted "Subject to subtitle B of the Consumer Financial Protection Act of 2010, compliance" for "Compliance" in introductory provisions.

Subsec. (a)(1). Pub. L. 111–203, §1084(5)(A)(ii), added par. (1) and struck out former par. (1) which read as follows: "section 8 of the Federal Deposit Insurance Act, in the case of—

"(A) national banks, and Federal branches and Federal agencies of foreign banks, by the Office of the Comptroller of the Currency;

"(B) member banks of the Federal Reserve System (other than national banks), branches and agencies of foreign banks (other than Federal branches, Federal agencies, and insured State branches of foreign banks), commercial lending companies owned or controlled by foreign banks, and organizations operating under section 25 or 25(a) of the Federal Reserve Act, by the Board; and

"(C) banks insured by the Federal Deposit Insurance Corporation (other than members of the Federal Reserve System) and insured State branches of foreign banks, by the Board of Directors of the Federal Deposit Insurance Corporation;".

Subsec. (a)(2) to (5). Pub. L. 111–203, §1084(5)(A)(ii)–(vii), added par. (5), redesignated former pars. (3) to (5) as (2) to (4), respectively, and struck out former par. (2) which read as follows: "section 8 of the Federal Deposit Insurance Act, by the Director of the Office of Thrift Supervision, in the case of a savings association the deposits of which are insured by the Federal Deposit Insurance Corporation;".

Subsec. (b). Pub. L. 111–203, §1084(5)(B), inserted "any of paragraphs (1) through (4) of" before "subsection (a)" in two places.

Subsec. (c). Pub. L. 111–203, §1084(5)(C), added subsec. (c) and struck out former subsec. (c). Prior to amendment, text read as follows: "Except to the extent that enforcement of the requirements imposed under this subchapter is specifically committed to some other Government agency under subsection (a) of this section, the Federal Trade Commission shall enforce such requirements. For the purpose of the exercise by the Federal Trade Commission of its functions and powers under the Federal Trade Commission Act, a violation of any requirement imposed under this subchapter shall be deemed a violation of a requirement imposed under that Act. All of the functions and powers of the Federal Trade Commission under the Federal Trade Commission Act are available to the Commission to enforce compliance by any person subject to the jurisdiction of the Commission with the requirements imposed under this subchapter, irrespective of whether that person is engaged in commerce or meets any other jurisdictional tests in the Federal Trade Commission Act."

1996—Subsec. (a)(4). Pub. L. 104–287 substituted "Secretary of Transportation" for "Civil Aeronautics Board".

1991—Subsec. (a). Pub. L. 102–242, §212(f)(2), inserted at end "The terms used in paragraph (1) that are not defined in this subchapter or otherwise defined in section 3(s) of the Federal Deposit Insurance Act (12 U.S.C. 1813(s)) shall have the meaning given to them in section 1(b) of the International Banking Act of 1978 (12 U.S.C. 3101)."

Pub. L. 102–242, §212(f)(1), added par. (1) and struck out former par. (1) which read as follows: "section 8 of the Federal Deposit Insurance Act, in the case of—

"(A) national banks, by the Comptroller of the Currency;

"(B) member banks of the Federal Reserve System (other than national banks), by the Board;

"(C) banks insured by the Federal Deposit Insurance Corporation (other than members of the Federal Reserve System), by the Board of Directors of the Federal Deposit Insurance Corporation;".

1989—Subsec. (a)(2). Pub. L. 101–73 amended par. (2) generally. Prior to amendment, par. (2) read as follows: "section 5(d) of the Home Owners' Loan Act of 1933, section 407 of the National Housing Act, and sections 6(i) and 17 of the Federal Home Loan Bank Act, by the Federal Home Loan Bank Board (acting directly or through the Federal Savings and Loan Insurance Corporation), in the case of any institution subject to any of those provisions;".

STATUTORY NOTES AND RELATED SUBSIDIARIES

EFFECTIVE DATE OF 2010 AMENDMENT

Amendment by Pub. L. 111–203 effective on the designated transfer date, see section 1100H of Pub. L. 111–203, set out as a note under section 552a of Title 5, Government Organization and Employees.

Functions vested in Administrator of National Credit Union Administration transferred and vested in National Credit Union Administration Board pursuant to section 1752a of Title 12, Banks and Banking.

[1] *So in original. Probably should be "; and".*

§1693o–1. Remittance transfers

(a) Disclosures required for remittance transfers

(1) In general

Each remittance transfer provider shall make disclosures as required under this section and in accordance with rules prescribed by the Bureau. Disclosures required under this section shall be in addition to any other disclosures applicable under this subchapter.

(2) Disclosures

Subject to rules prescribed by the Bureau, a remittance transfer provider shall provide, in writing and in a form that the sender may keep, to each sender requesting a remittance transfer, as applicable to the transaction—

(A) at the time at which the sender requests a remittance transfer to be initiated, and prior to the sender making any payment in connection with the remittance transfer, a disclosure describing—

(i) the amount of currency that will be received by the designated recipient, using the values of the currency into which the funds will be exchanged;

(ii) the amount of transfer and any other fees charged by the remittance transfer provider for the remittance transfer; and

(iii) any exchange rate to be used by the remittance transfer provider for the remittance transfer, to the nearest 1/100th of a point; and

(B) at the time at which the sender makes payment in connection with the remittance transfer—

(i) a receipt showing—

(I) the information described in subparagraph (A);

(II) the promised date of delivery to the designated recipient; and

(III) the name and either the telephone number or the address of the designated recipient, if either the telephone number or the address of the designated recipient is provided by the sender; and

(ii) a statement containing—

(I) information about the rights of the sender under this section regarding the resolution of errors; and

(II) appropriate contact information for—

(aa) the remittance transfer provider; and

(bb) the State agency that regulates the remittance transfer provider and the Bureau, including the toll-free telephone number established under section 5493 of title 12.

(3) Requirements relating to disclosures

With respect to each disclosure required to be provided under paragraph (2) a remittance transfer provider shall—

(A) provide an initial notice and receipt, as required by subparagraphs (A) and (B) of paragraph (2), and an error resolution statement, as required by subsection (d), that clearly and conspicuously describe the information required to be disclosed therein; and

(B) with respect to any transaction that a sender conducts electronically, comply with the Electronic Signatures in Global and National Commerce Act (15 U.S.C. 7001 et seq.).

(4) Exception for disclosures of amount received

(A) In general

Subject to the rules prescribed by the Bureau, and except as provided under subparagraph (B), the disclosures required regarding the amount of currency that will be received by the designated recipient shall be deemed to be accurate, so long as the disclosures provide a reasonably accurate estimate of the foreign currency to be received. This paragraph shall apply only to a remittance transfer provider who is an insured depository institution, as defined in section 1813 of title 12, or an insured credit union, as defined in section 1752 of title 12, and if—

(i) a remittance transfer is conducted through a demand deposit, savings deposit, or other asset account that the sender holds with such remittance transfer provider; and

(ii) at the time at which the sender requests the transaction, the remittance transfer provider is unable to know, for reasons beyond its control, the amount of currency that will be made available to the designated recipient.

(B) Deadline

The application of subparagraph (A) shall terminate 5 years after July 21, 2010, unless the Bureau determines that termination of such provision would negatively affect the ability of remittance transfer providers described in subparagraph (A) to send remittances to locations in foreign countries, in which case, the Bureau may, by rule, extend the application of subparagraph (A) to not longer than 10 years after July 21, 2010.

(5) Exemption authority

The Bureau may, by rule, permit a remittance transfer provider to satisfy the requirements of—

(A) paragraph (2)(A) orally, if the transaction is conducted entirely by telephone;

(B) paragraph (2)(B), in the case of a transaction conducted entirely by telephone, by mailing the disclosures required under such subparagraph to the sender, not later than 1 business day after the date on which the transaction is conducted, or by including such documents in the next periodic statement, if the telephone transaction is conducted through a demand deposit, savings deposit, or other asset account that the sender holds with the remittance transfer provider;

(C) subparagraphs (A) and (B) of paragraph (2) together in one written disclosure, but only to the extent that the information provided in accordance with paragraph (3)(A) is accurate at the time at which payment is made in connection with the subject remittance transfer; and

(D) paragraph (2)(A), without compliance with section 101(c) of the Electronic Signatures in Global Commerce Act [15 U.S.C. 7001(c)], if a sender initiates the transaction electronically and the information is displayed electronically in a manner that the sender can keep.

(6) Storefront and Internet notices

(A) In general

(i) Prominent posting

Subject to subparagraph (B), the Bureau may prescribe rules to require a remittance transfer provider to prominently post, and timely update, a notice describing a model remittance transfer for one or more amounts, as the Bureau may determine, which notice shall show the amount of currency that will be received by the designated recipient, using the values of the currency into which the funds will be exchanged.

(ii) Onsite displays

The Bureau may require the notice prescribed under this subparagraph to be displayed in every physical storefront location owned or controlled by the remittance transfer provider.

(iii) Internet notices

Subject to paragraph (3), the Bureau shall prescribe rules to require a remittance transfer provider that provides remittance transfers via the Internet to provide a notice, comparable to a storefront notice described in this subparagraph, located on the home page or landing page (with respect to such remittance transfer services) owned or controlled by the remittance transfer provider.

(iv) Rulemaking authority

In prescribing rules under this subparagraph, the Bureau may impose standards or requirements regarding the provision of the storefront and Internet notices required under this subparagraph and the provision of the disclosures required under paragraphs (2) and (3).

(B) Study and analysis

Prior to proposing rules under subparagraph (A), the Bureau shall undertake appropriate studies and analyses, which shall be consistent with section 1693b(a)(2) of this title, and may include an advanced notice of proposed rulemaking, to determine whether a storefront notice or Internet notice facilitates the ability of a consumer—

(i) to compare prices for remittance transfers; and

(ii) to understand the types and amounts of any fees or costs imposed on remittance transfers.

(b) Foreign language disclosures

The disclosures required under this section shall be made in English and in each of the foreign languages principally used by the remittance transfer provider, or any of its agents, to advertise, solicit, or market, either orally or in writing, at that office.

(c) Regulations regarding transfers to certain nations

If the Bureau determines that a recipient nation does not legally allow, or the method by which transactions are made in the recipient country do not allow, a remittance transfer provider to know the amount of currency that will be received by the designated recipient, the Bureau may prescribe rules (not later than 18 months after July 21, 2010) addressing the issue, which rules shall include standards for a remittance transfer provider to provide—

(1) a receipt that is consistent with subsections (a) and (b); and

(2) a reasonably accurate estimate of the foreign currency to be received, based on the rate provided to the sender by the remittance transfer provider at the time at which the transaction was initiated by the sender.

(d) Remittance transfer errors

(1) Error resolution

(A) In general

If a remittance transfer provider receives oral or written notice from the sender within 180 days of the promised date of delivery that an error occurred with respect to a remittance transfer, including the amount of currency designated in subsection (a)(3)(A) that was to be sent to the designated recipient of the remittance transfer, using the values of the currency into which the funds should have been exchanged, but was not made available to the designated recipient in the foreign country, the remittance transfer provider shall resolve the error pursuant to this subsection and investigate the reason for the error.

(B) Remedies

Not later than 90 days after the date of receipt of a notice from the sender pursuant to subparagraph (A), the remittance transfer provider shall, as applicable to the error and as designated by the sender—

(i) refund to the sender the total amount of funds tendered by the sender in connection with the remittance transfer which was not properly transmitted;

(ii) make available to the designated recipient, without additional cost to the designated recipient or to the sender, the amount appropriate to resolve the error;

(iii) provide such other remedy, as determined appropriate by rule of the Bureau for the protection of senders; or

(iv) provide written notice to the sender that there was no error with an explanation responding to the specific complaint of the sender.

(2) Rules

The Bureau shall establish, by rule issued not later than 18 months after July 21, 2010, clear and appropriate standards for remittance transfer providers with respect to error resolution relating to remittance transfers, to protect senders from such errors. Standards prescribed under this paragraph shall include appropriate standards regarding record keeping, as required, including documentation—

(A) of the complaint of the sender;

(B) that the sender provides the remittance transfer provider with respect to the alleged error; and

(C) of the findings of the remittance transfer provider regarding the investigation of the alleged error that the sender brought to their attention.

(3) Cancellation and refund policy rules

Not later than 18 months after July 21, 2010, the Bureau shall issue final rules regarding appropriate remittance transfer cancellation and refund policies for consumers.

(e) Applicability of this subchapter

(1) In general

A remittance transfer that is not an electronic fund transfer, as defined in section 1693a of this title, shall not be subject to any of the provisions of sections 1693c through 1693k of this title. A remittance transfer that is an electronic fund transfer, as defined in section 1693a of this title, shall be subject to all provisions of this subchapter, except for section 1693f of this title, that are otherwise applicable to electronic fund transfers under this subchapter.

(2) Rule of construction

Nothing in this section shall be construed—

(A) to affect the application to any transaction, to any remittance provider, or to any other person of any of the provisions of subchapter II of chapter 53 of title 31, section 1829b of title 12, or chapter 2 of title I of Public Law 91–508 (12 U.S.C. 1951–1959), or any regulations promulgated thereunder; or

(B) to cause any fund transfer that would not otherwise be treated as such under paragraph (1) to be treated as an electronic fund transfer, or as otherwise subject to this subchapter, for the purposes of any of the provisions referred to in subparagraph (A) or any regulations promulgated thereunder.

(f) Acts of agents

(1) In general

A remittance transfer provider shall be liable for any violation of this section by any agent, authorized delegate, or person affiliated with such provider, when such agent, authorized delegate, or affiliate acts for that remittance transfer provider.

(2) Obligations of remittance transfer providers

The Bureau shall prescribe rules to implement appropriate standards or conditions of, liability of a remittance transfer provider, including a provider who acts through an agent or authorized delegate. An agency charged with enforcing the requirements of this section, or rules prescribed by the Bureau under this section, may consider, in any action or other proceeding against a remittance transfer provider, the extent to which the provider had established and maintained policies or procedures for compliance, including policies, procedures, or other appropriate oversight measures designed to assure compliance by an agent or authorized delegate acting for such provider.

(g) Definitions

As used in this section—

(1) the term "designated recipient" means any person located in a foreign country and identified by the sender as the authorized recipient of a remittance transfer to be made by a remittance transfer provider, except that a designated recipient shall not be deemed to be a consumer for purposes of this chapter;

(2) the term "remittance transfer"—

(A) means the electronic (as defined in section 106(2) of the Electronic Signatures in Global and National Commerce Act (15 U.S.C. 7006(2))) transfer of funds requested by a sender located in any State to a designated recipient that is initiated by a remittance transfer provider, whether or not the sender holds an account with the remittance transfer provider or whether or not the remittance transfer is also an electronic fund transfer, as defined in section 1693a of this title; and

(B) does not include a transfer described in subparagraph (A) in an amount that is equal to or lesser than the amount of a small-value transaction determined, by rule, to be excluded from the requirements under section 1693d(a) of this title;

(3) the term "remittance transfer provider" means any person or financial institution that provides remittance transfers for a consumer in the normal course of its business, whether or not the consumer holds an account with such person or financial institution; and

(4) the term "sender" means a consumer who requests a remittance provider to send a remittance transfer for the consumer to a designated recipient.

(Pub. L. 90–321, title IX, §919, as added and amended Pub. L. 111–203, title X, §§1073(a)(4), 1084(1), July 21, 2010, 124 Stat. 2060, 2081.)

EDITORIAL NOTES

REFERENCES IN TEXT

The Electronic Signatures in Global and National Commerce Act, referred to in subsec. (a)(3)(B), is Pub. L. 106–229, June 30, 2000, 114 Stat. 464, which is classified principally to chapter 96 (§7001 et seq.) of this title. For complete classification of this Act to the Code, see Short Title note set out under section 7001 of this title and Tables.

Chapter 2 of title I of Public Law 91–508, referred to in subsec. (e)(2)(A), is chapter 2 (§§121–129) of title I of Pub. L. 91–508, Oct. 26, 1970, 84 Stat. 1116, which is classified generally to chapter 21 (§1951 et seq.) of Title 12, Banks and Banking. For complete classification of chapter 2 of title I of the Act to the Code, see Tables.

PRIOR PROVISIONS

A prior section 919 of Pub. L. 90–321 was renumbered section 921 and is classified to section 1693p of this title.

Another prior section 919 of Pub. L. 90–321 was renumbered section 922 and is classified to section 1693q of this title.

AMENDMENTS

2010—Pub. L. 111–203, §1084(1), substituted "Bureau" for "Board" wherever appearing.

STATUTORY NOTES AND RELATED SUBSIDIARIES

EFFECTIVE DATE OF 2010 AMENDMENT

Amendment by section 1084(1) of Pub. L. 111–203 effective on the designated transfer date, see section 1100H of Pub. L. 111–203, set out as a note under section 552a of Title 5, Government Organization and Employees.

EFFECTIVE DATE

Section effective 1 day after July 21, 2010, except as otherwise provided, see section 4 of Pub. L. 111–203, set out as a note under section 5301 of Title 12, Banks and Banking.

§1693*o*–2. Reasonable fees and rules for payment card transactions

(a) Reasonable interchange transaction fees for electronic debit transactions

(1) Regulatory authority over interchange transaction fees

The Board may prescribe regulations, pursuant to section 553 of title 5, regarding any interchange transaction fee that an issuer may receive or charge with respect to an electronic debit transaction, to implement this subsection (including related definitions), and to prevent circumvention or evasion of this subsection.

(2) Reasonable interchange transaction fees

The amount of any interchange transaction fee that an issuer may receive or charge with respect to an electronic debit transaction shall be reasonable and proportional to the cost incurred by the issuer with respect to the transaction.

(3) Rulemaking required

(A) In general

The Board shall prescribe regulations in final form not later than 9 months after July 21, 2010, to establish standards for assessing whether the amount of any interchange transaction fee described in paragraph (2) is reasonable and proportional to the cost incurred by the issuer with respect to the transaction.

(B) Information collection

The Board may require any issuer (or agent of an issuer) or payment card network to provide the Board with such information as may be necessary to carry out the provisions of this subsection and the Board, in issuing rules under subparagraph (A) and on at least a bi-annual basis thereafter, shall disclose such aggregate or summary information concerning the costs incurred, and interchange transaction fees charged or received, by issuers or payment card networks in connection with the authorization, clearance or settlement of electronic debit transactions as the Board considers appropriate and in the public interest.

(4) Considerations; consultation

In prescribing regulations under paragraph (3)(A), the Board shall—
  (A) consider the functional similarity between—
    (i) electronic debit transactions; and
    (ii) checking transactions that are required within the Federal Reserve bank system to clear at par;

  (B) distinguish between—
    (i) the incremental cost incurred by an issuer for the role of the issuer in the authorization, clearance, or settlement of a particular electronic debit transaction, which cost shall be considered under paragraph (2); and
    (ii) other costs incurred by an issuer which are not specific to a particular electronic debit transaction, which costs shall not be considered under paragraph (2); and

  (C) consult, as appropriate, with the Comptroller of the Currency, the Board of Directors of the Federal Deposit Insurance Corporation, the Director of the Office of Thrift Supervision, the National Credit Union Administration Board, the Administrator of the Small Business Administration, and the Director of the Bureau of Consumer Financial Protection.

(5) Adjustments to interchange transaction fees for fraud prevention costs

(A) Adjustments

The Board may allow for an adjustment to the fee amount received or charged by an issuer under paragraph (2), if—
    (i) such adjustment is reasonably necessary to make allowance for costs incurred by the issuer in preventing fraud in relation to electronic debit transactions involving that issuer; and
    (ii) the issuer complies with the fraud-related standards established by the Board under subparagraph (B), which standards shall—
      (I) be designed to ensure that any fraud-related adjustment of the issuer is limited to the amount described in clause (i) and takes into account any fraud-related reimbursements (including amounts from charge-backs) received from consumers, merchants, or payment card networks in relation to electronic debit transactions involving the issuer; and
      (II) require issuers to take effective steps to reduce the occurrence of, and costs from, fraud in relation to electronic debit transactions, including through the development and implementation of cost-effective fraud prevention technology.

(B) Rulemaking required

(i) In general

The Board shall prescribe regulations in final form not later than 9 months after July 21, 2010, to establish standards for making adjustments under this paragraph.

(ii) Factors for consideration

In issuing the standards and prescribing regulations under this paragraph, the Board shall consider—
    (I) the nature, type, and occurrence of fraud in electronic debit transactions;

(II) the extent to which the occurrence of fraud depends on whether authorization in an electronic debit transaction is based on signature, PIN, or other means;

(III) the available and economical means by which fraud on electronic debit transactions may be reduced;

(IV) the fraud prevention and data security costs expended by each party involved in electronic debit transactions (including consumers, persons who accept debit cards as a form of payment, financial institutions, retailers and payment card networks);

(V) the costs of fraudulent transactions absorbed by each party involved in such transactions (including consumers, persons who accept debit cards as a form of payment, financial institutions, retailers and payment card networks);

(VI) the extent to which interchange transaction fees have in the past reduced or increased incentives for parties involved in electronic debit transactions to reduce fraud on such transactions; and

(VII) such other factors as the Board considers appropriate.

(6) Exemption for small issuers

(A) In general

This subsection shall not apply to any issuer that, together with its affiliates, has assets of less than $10,000,000,000, and the Board shall exempt such issuers from regulations prescribed under paragraph (3)(A).

(B) Definition

For purposes of this paragraph, the term "issuer" shall be limited to the person holding the asset account that is debited through an electronic debit transaction.

(7) Exemption for government-administered payment programs and reloadable prepaid cards

(A) In general

This subsection shall not apply to an interchange transaction fee charged or received with respect to an electronic debit transaction in which a person uses—

(i) a debit card or general-use prepaid card that has been provided to a person pursuant to a Federal, State or local government-administered payment program, in which the person may only use the debit card or general-use prepaid card to transfer or debit funds, monetary value, or other assets that have been provided pursuant to such program; or

(ii) a plastic card, payment code, or device that is—

(I) linked to funds, monetary value, or assets which are purchased or loaded on a prepaid basis;

(II) not issued or approved for use to access or debit any account held by or for the benefit of the card holder (other than a subaccount or other method of recording or tracking funds purchased or loaded on the card on a prepaid basis);

(III) redeemable at multiple, unaffiliated merchants or service providers, or automated teller machines;

(IV) used to transfer or debit funds, monetary value, or other assets; and

(V) reloadable and not marketed or labeled as a gift card or gift certificate.

(B) Exception

Notwithstanding subparagraph (A), after the end of the 1-year period beginning on the effective date provided in paragraph (9), this subsection shall apply to an interchange transaction fee charged or received with respect to an electronic debit transaction described in subparagraph (A)(i) in which a person uses a general-use prepaid card, or an electronic debit transaction described in subparagraph (A)(ii), if any of the following fees may be charged to a person with respect to the card:

(i) A fee for an overdraft, including a shortage of funds or a transaction processed for an amount exceeding the account balance.

(ii) A fee imposed by the issuer for the first withdrawal per month from an automated teller machine that is part of the issuer's designated automated teller machine network.

(C) Definition

For purposes of subparagraph (B), the term "designated automated teller machine network" means either—

(i) all automated teller machines identified in the name of the issuer; or

(ii) any network of automated teller machines identified by the issuer that provides reasonable and convenient access to the issuer's customers.

(D) Reporting

Beginning 12 months after July 21, 2010, the Board shall annually provide a report to the Congress regarding —

(i) the prevalence of the use of general-use prepaid cards in Federal, State or local government-administered payment programs; and

(ii) the interchange transaction fees and cardholder fees charged with respect to the use of such general-use prepaid cards.

(8) Regulatory authority over network fees

(A) In general

The Board may prescribe regulations, pursuant to section 553 of title 5, regarding any network fee.

(B) Limitation

The authority under subparagraph (A) to prescribe regulations shall be limited to regulations to ensure that—

(i) a network fee is not used to directly or indirectly compensate an issuer with respect to an electronic debit transaction; and

(ii) a network fee is not used to circumvent or evade the restrictions of this subsection and regulations prescribed under such subsection.

(C) Rulemaking required

The Board shall prescribe regulations in final form before the end of the 9-month period beginning on July 21, 2010, to carry out the authorities provided under subparagraph (A).

(9) Effective date

This subsection shall take effect at the end of the 12-month period beginning on July 21, 2010.

(b) Limitation on payment card network restrictions

(1) Prohibitions against exclusivity arrangements

(A) No exclusive network

The Board shall, before the end of the 1-year period beginning on July 21, 2010, prescribe regulations providing that an issuer or payment card network shall not directly or through any agent, processor, or licensed member of a payment card network, by contract, requirement, condition, penalty, or otherwise, restrict the number of payment card networks on which an electronic debit transaction may be processed to—

(i) 1 such network; or

(ii) 2 or more such networks which are owned, controlled, or otherwise operated by —

(I) affiliated persons; or

(II) networks affiliated with such issuer.

(B) No routing restrictions

The Board shall, before the end of the 1-year period beginning on July 21, 2010, prescribe regulations providing that an issuer or payment card network shall not, directly or through any agent, processor, or licensed member of the network, by contract, requirement, condition, penalty, or otherwise, inhibit the ability of any person who accepts debit cards for payments to direct the routing of electronic debit transactions for processing over any payment card network that may process such transactions.

(2) Limitation on restrictions on offering discounts for use of a form of payment

(A) In general

A payment card network shall not, directly or through any agent, processor, or licensed member of the network, by contract, requirement, condition, penalty, or otherwise, inhibit the ability of any person to provide a discount or in-kind incentive for payment by the use of cash, checks, debit cards, or credit cards to the extent that—

(i) in the case of a discount or in-kind incentive for payment by the use of debit cards, the discount or in-kind incentive does not differentiate on the basis of the issuer or the payment card network;

(ii) in the case of a discount or in-kind incentive for payment by the use of credit cards, the discount or in-kind incentive does not differentiate on the basis of the issuer or the payment card network; and

(iii) to the extent required by Federal law and applicable State law, such discount or in-kind incentive is offered to all prospective buyers and disclosed clearly and conspicuously.

(B) Lawful discounts

For purposes of this paragraph, the network may not penalize any person for the providing of a discount that is in compliance with Federal law and applicable State law.

(3) Limitation on restrictions on setting transaction minimums or maximums

(A) In general

A payment card network shall not, directly or through any agent, processor, or licensed member of the network, by contract, requirement, condition, penalty, or otherwise, inhibit the ability—

(i) of any person to set a minimum dollar value for the acceptance by that person of credit cards, to the extent that—

(I) such minimum dollar value does not differentiate between issuers or between payment card networks; and

(II) such minimum dollar value does not exceed $10.00; or

(ii) of any Federal agency or institution of higher education to set a maximum dollar value for the acceptance by that Federal agency or institution of higher education of credit cards, to the extent that such maximum dollar value does not differentiate between issuers or between payment card networks.

(B) Increase in minimum dollar amount

The Board may, by regulation prescribed pursuant to section 553 of title 5, increase the amount of the dollar value listed in subparagraph (A)(i)(II).

(4) Rule of construction

No provision of this subsection shall be construed to authorize any person—

(A) to discriminate between debit cards within a payment card network on the basis of the issuer that issued the debit card; or

(B) to discriminate between credit cards within a payment card network on the basis of the issuer that issued the credit card.

(c) Definitions

For purposes of this section, the following definitions shall apply:

(1) Affiliate

The term "affiliate" means any company that controls, is controlled by, or is under common control with another company.

(2) Debit card

The term "debit card"—

(A) means any card, or other payment code or device, issued or approved for use through a payment card network to debit an asset account (regardless of the purpose for which the account is established), whether authorization is based on signature, PIN, or other means;

(B) includes a general-use prepaid card, as that term is defined in section 1693l–1(a)(2)(A) of this title; and

(C) does not include paper checks.

(3) Credit card

The term "credit card" has the same meaning as in section 1602 of this title.

(4) Discount

The term "discount"—

(A) means a reduction made from the price that customers are informed is the regular price; and

(B) does not include any means of increasing the price that customers are informed is the regular price.

(5) Electronic debit transaction

The term "electronic debit transaction" means a transaction in which a person uses a debit card.

(6) Federal agency

The term "Federal agency" means—

(A) an agency (as defined in section 101 of title 31); and

(B) a Government corporation (as defined in section 103 of title 5).

(7) Institution of higher education

The term "institution of higher education" has the same meaning as in 1001 [1] and 1002 of title 20.

(8) Interchange transaction fee

The term "interchange transaction fee" means any fee established, charged or received by a payment card network for the purpose of compensating an issuer for its involvement in an electronic debit transaction.

(9) Issuer

The term "issuer" means any person who issues a debit card, or credit card, or the agent of such person with respect to such card.

(10) Network fee

The term "network fee" means any fee charged and received by a payment card network with respect to an electronic debit transaction, other than an interchange transaction fee.

(11) Payment card network

The term "payment card network" means an entity that directly, or through licensed members, processors, or agents, provides the proprietary services, infrastructure, and software that route information and data to conduct debit card or credit card transaction authorization, clearance, and settlement, and that a person uses in order to accept as a form of payment a brand of debit card, credit card or other device that may be used to carry out debit or credit transactions.

(d) Enforcement

(1) In general

Compliance with the requirements imposed under this section shall be enforced under section 1693o of this title.

(2) Exception

Sections 1693m and 1693n of this title shall not apply with respect to this section or the requirements imposed pursuant to this section.

(Pub. L. 90–321, title IX, §920, as added Pub. L. 111–203, title X, §1075(a)(2), July 21, 2010, 124 Stat. 2068.)

EDITORIAL NOTES

PRIOR PROVISIONS

A prior section 920 of Pub. L. 90–321 was renumbered section 921 and is classified to section 1693p of this title.

Two other prior sections 920 of Pub. L. 90–321 were renumbered section 922 and are classified to sections 1693q and 1693r of this title.

STATUTORY NOTES AND RELATED SUBSIDIARIES

EFFECTIVE DATE

Section effective 1 day after July 21, 2010, except as otherwise provided, see section 4 of Pub. L. 111–203, set out as a note under section 5301 of Title 12, Banks and Banking.

[1] So in original. Probably should be preceded by "sections".

§1693p. Reports to Congress

(a) Not later than twelve months after the effective date of this subchapter and at one-year intervals thereafter, the Bureau shall make reports to the Congress concerning the administration of its functions under this subchapter, including such recommendations as the Bureau deems necessary and appropriate. In addition, each report of the Bureau shall include its assessment of the extent to which compliance with this subchapter is being achieved, and a summary of the enforcement actions taken under section 1693o [1] of this title. In such report, the Bureau shall particularly address the effects of this subchapter on the costs and benefits to financial institutions and consumers, on competition, on the introduction of new technology, on the operations of financial institutions, and on the adequacy of consumer protection.

(b) In the exercise of its functions under this subchapter, the Bureau may obtain upon request the views of any other Federal agency which, in the judgment of the Bureau, exercises regulatory or supervisory functions with respect to any class of persons subject to this subchapter.

(Pub. L. 90–321, title IX, §921, formerly §918, as added Pub. L. 95–630, title XX, §2001, Nov. 10, 1978, 92 Stat. 3740; amended Pub. L. 97–375, title II, §209(a), Dec. 21, 1982, 96 Stat. 1825; renumbered §919, Pub. L. 111–24, title IV, §401(1), May 22, 2009, 123 Stat. 1751; renumbered §920, renumbered §921, and amended Pub. L. 111–203, title X, §§1073(a)(3), 1075(a)(1), 1084(1), July 21, 2010, 124 Stat. 2060, 2068, 2081.)

EDITORIAL NOTES

REFERENCES IN TEXT

For effective date of this subchapter, referred to in subsec. (a), see section 921 of Pub. L. 90–321, set out as an Effective Date note under section 1693 of this title.

Section 1693o of this title, referred to in subsec. (a), was in the original "section 917 of this title", and was translated as meaning section 918 of title I of Pub. L. 90–321 to reflect the probable intent of Congress and the renumbering of section 917 of title I of Pub. L. 90–321 as section 918 by Pub. L. 111–24, title IV, §401(1), May 22, 2009, 123 Stat. 1751.

CODIFICATION

Renumbering of section 918 of Pub. L. 90–321 as section 919 by section 401(1) of Pub. L. 111–24 was executed prior to the renumberings of section 919 of Pub. L. 90–321 as section 920 and then as section 921 by sections 1073(a)(3) and 1075(a)(1) of Pub. L. 111–203 as the probable intent of Congress, notwithstanding section 403 of Pub. L. 111–24, set out as an Effective Date note under section 1693l–1 of this title and section 4 of Pub. L. 111–203, set out as an Effective Date note under section 5301 of Title 12, Banks and Banking, which provided that the renumbering by Pub. L. 111–24 was effective 15 months after May 22, 2009, and the renumberings by Pub. L. 111–203 were effective 1 day after July 21, 2010.

PRIOR PROVISIONS

Two prior sections 921 of Pub. L. 90–321 were renumbered section 922 and are classified to sections 1693q and 1693r of this title.

Another prior section 921 of Pub. L. 90–321 was renumbered section 923 and is classified as an Effective Date note under section 1693 of this title.

AMENDMENTS

2010—Pub. L. 111–203, §1084(1), substituted "Bureau" for "Board" wherever appearing.

1982—Subsec. (a). Pub. L. 97–375 struck out requirement that the Attorney General make a report on the same terms as the Board, and that such report also contain an analysis of the impact of this subchapter on the operation, workload, and efficiency of the Federal courts, and substituted "necessary and appropriate" for "necessary or appropriate".

STATUTORY NOTES AND RELATED SUBSIDIARIES

EFFECTIVE DATE OF 2010 AMENDMENT

Amendment by section 1084(1) of Pub. L. 111–203 effective on the designated transfer date, see section 1100H of Pub. L. 111–203, set out as a note under section 552a of Title 5, Government Organization and Employees.

1 *See References in Text note below.*

§1693q. Relation to State laws

This subchapter does not annul, alter, or affect the laws of any State relating to electronic fund transfers, dormancy fees, inactivity charges or fees, service fees, or expiration dates of gift certificates, store gift cards, or general-use prepaid cards, except to the extent that those laws are inconsistent with the provisions of this subchapter, and then only to the extent of the inconsistency. A State law is not inconsistent with this subchapter if the protection such law affords any consumer is greater than the protection afforded by this subchapter. The Bureau shall, upon its own motion or upon the request of any financial institution, State, or other interested party, submitted in accordance with procedures prescribed in regulations of the Bureau, determine whether a State requirement is inconsistent or affords greater protection. If the Bureau determines that a State requirement is inconsistent, financial institutions shall incur no liability under the law of that State for a good faith failure to comply with that law, notwithstanding that such determination is subsequently amended, rescinded, or determined by judicial or other authority to be invalid for any reason. This subchapter does not extend the applicability of any such law to any class of persons or transactions to which it would not otherwise apply.

(Pub. L. 90–321, title IX, §922, formerly §919, as added Pub. L. 95–630, title XX, §2001, Nov. 10, 1978, 92 Stat. 3741; renumbered §920 and amended Pub. L. 111–24, title IV, §§401(1), 402, May 22, 2009, 123 Stat. 1751, 1754; renumbered §921, renumbered §922, and amended Pub. L. 111–203, title X, §§1073(a)(3), 1075(a)(1), 1084(1), July 21, 2010, 124 Stat. 2060, 2068, 2081.)

EDITORIAL NOTES

CODIFICATION

Another section 922 of Pub. L. 90–321 is classified to section 1693r of this title.

Renumbering of section 919 of Pub. L. 90–321 as section 920 by section 401(1) of Pub. L. 111–24 was executed prior to the renumberings of section 920 of Pub. L. 90–321 as section 921 and then as section 922 by sections 1073(a)(3) and 1075(a)(1) of Pub. L. 111–203 as the probable intent of Congress, notwithstanding section 403 of Pub. L. 111–24, set out as an Effective Date note under section 1693l–1 of this title and section 4 of Pub. L. 111–203, set out as an Effective Date note under section 5301 of Title 12, Banks and Banking, which provided that the renumbering by Pub. L. 111–24 was effective 15 months after May 22, 2009, and the renumberings by Pub. L. 111–203 were effective 1 day after July 21, 2010.

PRIOR PROVISIONS

A prior section 922 of Pub. L. 90–321 was renumbered section 923 and is classified as an Effective Date note under section 1693 of this title.

AMENDMENTS

2010—Pub. L. 111–203, §1084(1), substituted "Bureau" for "Board" wherever appearing.

2009—Pub. L. 111–24, §402, inserted "dormancy fees, inactivity charges or fees, service fees, or expiration dates of gift certificates, store gift cards, or general-use prepaid cards," after "electronic fund transfers,".

EFFECTIVE DATE OF 2010 AMENDMENT

Amendment by section 1084(1) of Pub. L. 111–203 effective on the designated transfer date, see section 1100H of Pub. L. 111–203, set out as a note under section 552a of Title 5, Government Organization and Employees.

EFFECTIVE DATE OF 2009 AMENDMENT

Amendment by Pub. L. 111–24 effective 15 months after May 22, 2009, see section 403 of Pub. L. 111–24, set out as an Effective Date note under section 1693l–1 of this title.

§1693r. Exemption for State regulation

The Bureau shall by regulation exempt from the requirements of this subchapter any class of electronic fund transfers within any State if the Bureau determines that under the law of that State that class of electronic fund transfers is subject to requirements substantially similar to those imposed by this subchapter, and that there is adequate provision for enforcement.

(Pub. L. 90–321, title IX, §922, formerly §920, as added Pub. L. 95–630, title XX, §2001, Nov. 10, 1978, 92 Stat. 3741; renumbered §921, Pub. L. 111–24, title IV, §401(1), May 22, 2009, 123 Stat. 1751; renumbered §922 and amended Pub. L. 111–203, title X, §§1073(a)(3), 1084(1), July 21, 2010, 124 Stat. 2060, 2081.)

CODIFICATION

Another section 922 of Pub. L. 90–321 is classified to section 1693q of this title.

Renumbering of section 920 of Pub. L. 90–321 as section 921 by section 401(1) of Pub. L. 111–24 was executed prior to the renumbering of section 921 of Pub. L. 90–321 as section 922 by section 1073(a)(3) of Pub. L. 111–203 as the probable intent of Congress, notwithstanding section 403 of Pub. L. 111–24, set out as an Effective Date note under section 1693l–1 of this title and section 4 of Pub. L. 111–203, set out as an Effective Date note under section 5301 of Title 12, Banks and Banking, which provided that the renumbering by Pub. L. 111–24 was effective 15 months after May 22, 2009, and the renumbering by Pub. L. 111–203 was effective 1 day after July 21, 2010.

PRIOR PROVISIONS

A prior section 922 of Pub. L. 90–321 was renumbered section 923 and is classified as an Effective Date note under section 1693 of this title.

AMENDMENTS

2010—Pub. L. 111–203, §1084(1), substituted "Bureau" for "Board" in two places.

EFFECTIVE DATE OF 2010 AMENDMENT

Amendment by section 1084(1) of Pub. L. 111–203 effective on the designated transfer date, see section 1100H of Pub. L. 111–203, set out as a note under section 552a of Title 5, Government Organization and Employees.

This marks the end of the Electronic Fund Transfer Act
15 U.S.C. §§ 1693–1693r

This edition is revised and current as of January 2024

2024 | Applied Legal Publications

Made in the USA
Las Vegas, NV
18 April 2024

88828363R00042